HISTORY AND THE

MORRIS DANCE

HISTORY AND THE
MORRIS DANCE

A look at morris dancing

from its earliest days until 1850

John Cutting

DANCE
BOOKS
Alton

Herga Morris
Grand Union Morris
Lord Paget's Morris

With many happy memories

© John Cutting, 2005

First published by Dance Books Ltd,
The Old Bakery, 4 Lenten Street, Alton
Hampshire GU34 1HG

ISBN:1 85273 108 7

A CIP catalogue record for this book
is available from the British Library

Printed and bound in Great Britain by Latimer Trend, Plymouth, Devon

CONTENTS

Picture credits

The author wishes to thank the following organisations who have granted permission for illustrations to appear in this book. Some made a charge for this permission and some did not.

Illustration p.17	The British Library	
Illustration p.79	The British Library	
Illustration p.104	The National Archives, Kew	

1a	MS. Bodl. 264, fol	84v (detail)	Bodleian Library, University of
1b		78r (detail)	Oxford
1d		129r (detail)	
1f		21v	

9	Douce Prints E. 2.6 (327A)
36	G. A. Staffs 4⁰7, insert at p.353

4, 8, 21, 33, 41   The British Museum

12, 13, 29   V &A Images /Victoria and Albert Museum

2   MS. IV F 21, fol. 146v (detail)   The University Library in Wroclaw, Poland

5   MS. 11770. i.l ; 7915. R. 9; lB. 3979 (detail) The British Library

24   Lancaster City Museums

28   Fitzwilliam Museum, Cambridge

30   Perth Museum and Art Gallery, Perth and Kinross Council, Scotland

35   Cheltenham Art Gallery and Museum

37   Buckinghamshire Archaeological Society

Substantial efforts have been made to trace and contact owners, or those who hold reproduction rights. In some cases these efforts have not been successful. The author apologises to anyone whose rights have been accidentally infringed by the publication of illustrations in this book.

CHAPTER 1

AN INTRODUCTION

Morris is real to its audience in a way that stage dance can never be, for dancer and watcher are on the same level and meet as equals. Thus, questions are easily asked: 'How old is it?' 'Why is it called Morris?' 'What is it for?'

A century and a half ago morris audiences probably watched and accepted the dancing as a natural part of the yearly round; but today, our ways of thought have been tailored by science and politics until we are less inclined to 'just accept'. Questions are put, and replies like, 'It's an old fertility ritual' or, 'It goes back to the Moors in Spain' have become traditional responses to queries that are not easy to answer sensibly. Many times have I been asked questions of this sort, and various have been the answers I have given. Every once in a while one enquirer will be more persistent than the rest and go on to ask, 'Where can I find out something about the background to morris?'

If such a person goes along to a local library, all he or she is likely to discover is a reprint of Cecil Sharp's *Morris Book*; while a little careful combing through the catalogues might possibly add the name of *The Espérance Morris Book* by Mary Neal. Both admirable works, but written by collectors to assist in the instruction of dancers during the first few, heady years of a folk dance revival before the First World War. Not really what our present enquirer is looking for. If he presses on, he may discover the world of the English Folk Dance and Song Society with their journal (referred to as *JEFDSS*), their magazine *English Dance and Song* and of course their library, the Vaughan Williams Memorial Library. He may also hear of The Morris Ring, a national body linking independent men's morris clubs and serving those clubs as a centre for the collection and dissemination of morris information. These discoveries will give him access to a mass of papers, articles and the like, sufficient to keep him reading for a year or more – but our enquirer wasn't looking for a research project! Let us suppose that what he really wanted was a single volume giving a straightforward picture of the beginnings and growth of morris dancing, together with enough historical background to give a sense of context. Here then, is the purpose that I hope this book will fulfil.

* * * * *

References to morris are not common in the historical record and even when they do turn up they are often little more than a simple mention of the name. Fortunately for us, a small handful of accounts from the sixteenth century onwards do expand to give a little more detail. Working through material of this sort I was first struck, and then amused, by a recurring idea: an idea that is most clearly expressed in the form, 'Morris isn't what it used to be: once it was great, but now all that's left are a few remnants'. Time and time again I came across this idea in all periods of writing. My amusement gave way to wondering whether, perhaps, this was a serious idea in fancy dress: a clue pointing to some element, some key vital to the understanding of morris. Arbeau, writing instructions for his pupil in 1589, says of the morris:

> . . . . this dance has fallen into disuse. I will only give you the melody and movements of one passage [presumably all that Arbeau knew]. As for the others you can learn them from those who are schooled therein although few such persons are to be found nowadays.

Three hundred and twenty years later Cecil Sharp's informants told an essentially similar story. It seems that the collecting of folk material has been a race with the undertaker from the very beginning.

A strong tendency to look back on days when things were better seems to come as standard equipment with the ordinary human brain. The Golden Age, Arcadia, The Good Old Days and Merrie England – all have grown up as refuges against the unpalatable reality of the present. I believe that this Golden Age Syndrome, which blends a small measure of history with a large dose of romantic invention, has got itself mixed up with the backward-looking element in morris. Whether or not this suggestion has any truth in it, the fact is clear that most opinions on early morris that have been expressed during the present folk dance revival lean more towards the fun of speculation than they do towards the discipline of evidence. By way of example I want to look first at the historical content of a paper written as recently as 1978 and circulated by The Morris Ring.

Consideration of what constitutes morris dancing leads the Author to identify four salient features [my comments in parentheses].

1) Morris is danced at a fixed time every year. [i.e. Christmas, New Year's Day, Plough Monday, Easter, Mayday, Whitsun or harvest time, according to locality; although why there should be this variety is not explained. It is commonly believed that morris is, or should be, seasonal, despite widespread evidence to the contrary.]

2

2) Morris dancers wear a special costume. [True.]
3) Morris is danced by men only. [This is obviously not true of the last eighty years. Say 'Morris dancer' to someone from Manchester and he or she will think automatically of a teenage girl and the carnival morris. To say, with the Author, 'Ah, but this is not true morris', is to follow a slippery path to a happy land where all evidence supports, and anything contrary is labelled 'invalid'.]
4) Morris is danced by small numbers. [True, although I dislike the secret-society overtones introduced by using the word 'fraternity'.]

From little more than these four premises we pass on to morris being a ritual: being a luck-bringing service to a community, promoting the cycle of the seasons. Before we have time to notice the gap in the pavement, it is implied that morris dancers may be 'the descendants through some 50 or 60 generations from a pre-Christian priesthood whose duty it was to carry out seasonal rituals on behalf of the whole community'. This points to around 600 AD (allowing 55 generations of 25 years), the darkest part of the Dark Ages in post-Roman Britain. Since the earliest reference to morris in England is 1458, the length of morris history has been casually increased by a factor of two and a half times! To be fair, he does go on to note the arrival of a foreign dance-form called moresque or morisca at the end of the fifteenth century (for which there is some evidence) and he sees this import beginning as an entertainment at court revels, then becoming an attraction in public processions and finally being added to parish entertainments and pageants (all good supportable stuff). Once the morisca had descended the social scale to this level, it blended with the pre-existing English ritual dance and the mixture took on the name of morris. Unfortunately this 'pre-existing English ritual dance' lacks any confirmation from evidence and so must be relegated to the level of 'convenient supposition'.

A second example, this time from the early days of the current morris revival:

> The characteristic of the processional form of the dance as performed by the living dancers to-day is a slow, dignified rhythmic movement, which is very marked in the Bampton (Oxon.) dancers, who have an unbroken tradition going back some hundreds of years.
>
> The set dances display a much more lively character and are characterised by wild leaps, twirlings round, hand-clapping, stick clashing, and the waving of handkerchiefs, so that we can easily imagine the present Morris as a descendant of the solemn processional up the

mountain-side to greet the morning sun, and the scenes of wild joy on the summit at the appearance of the source of light and life to his waiting worshippers.

Mary Neal in *English Folk-Song and Dance*, 1915.

Both these authors have done tremendous work for the furtherance of morris and they have the sincere respect of most of us (which is why the first one is not identified here) but they share, together with so many others, an Achilles heel when it comes to morris history. It is an objective of this book to present enough of the facts to help the reader enjoy these flights of fancy without being swept away by them. The work that follows will not be devoid of speculation, but I intend to keep it under some control and ensure that it is clearly labelled.

* * * * *

Preliminary thoughts about a history of morris soon uncover two fundamental problems: problems which have impressed a particular shape upon the surviving evidence. The first one revolves around the question, 'How do you write down a dance?' The second is best summed up in the grossly oversimplified statement, 'History is about kings and wars, not about the pastimes of ordinary people'.

Watch a set of Cotswold morris dances – then go home and write down what you have seen. You could record the date, the time and the place without difficulty and describe whether it was a formal display at a festival, or a chance encounter in the street. If you were sufficiently interested you could go on to describe the dress (or 'kit' as it is now usually called) and perhaps mention clashing sticks or waving handkerchiefs. If a Fool or Hobby-horse had been in attendance then your account could expand in this direction, for these are easy things to describe. Add to this something about the musician, the instrument and the tunes, and you have an excellent record of the event – the only thing missing is the dance.

This description of yours will follow a pattern that soon becomes familiar when we read historical records, and it focuses our attention onto the fact that it is, and always has been, very difficult to set down on paper the steps, figures and movements of a dance. Ciné and video cameras can now ease the work of a dance collector, but before our day, anybody who wanted to record a dance had to learn or invent a system of dance notation. It is therefore not very surprising when we find out that the handful of people who combined the intelligence, the inclination and the time to master such a system were, generally speaking, either unaware of morris dancing, or simply not interested in what they would regard as a lower-class sport.

So it comes about that when we look for morris dances that are noted down in sufficient detail for us to reconstruct a performance, we find a single, poor-quality example in 1589 – then nothing else until 1907. For in 1907, Cecil Sharp with Herbert MacIlwaine (Musical Director of the Espérance Girls' Club) devised a form of notation designed specifically for writing down morris dances, and from this date onward we have a large amount of material available for study.

Many of the men who described and demonstrated dances for Cecil Sharp and the other collectors were quite elderly, and some of them had not danced for thirty or forty years. So, taking these circumstances into account, it seems reasonable to accept that the memories of these old men, aided by the collectors' skill, have given us notation that fairly represents the morris of 1870, perhaps 1860, or, as an extreme possibility, 1850. But before that, nothing – no notation of dance, apart from Arbeau's description of heel taps in 1589. Thus, the history of morris before 1850 has to be handled as best we can with very little information about what the dancers were actually doing.

There is a persuasive school of thought which argues that folk customs have great persistence and endure for long periods of time with little or no change. This school might well say that, if we know how morris was danced in 1850, then it cannot have been very different in 1840 – and upon receiving a grudging nod from the listener, add – or 1800 : or 1700 : or ..... It is true to say that some strands of folk tradition do show great longevity, but there is also plenty of evidence for conscious modification and outright invention among these so-called 'traditional' activities. People value their traditions and there are some groups who are not above creating a few new ones to meet the demand. In addition to this I am fairly sure that a process of 'deliberate forgetting' is sometimes employed to convert a new idea into an 'old custom of forgotten origin' in a remarkably short space of time. Possibilities of this sort must always be held in mind whenever we project images of morris backwards into the past.

Let us now have a look at the second problem: the one that has to do with the nature of history. The point I want to make is best introduced by considering the way historical records of village pastimes came to be noted down in the first place.

(As an aside, let us remind ourselves that most of our practical information about morris in its 'traditional' setting comes from the Cotswold villages in the third quarter of the nineteenth century, when the dance was a matter for labourers and artisans. Most people project this image backwards and see morris as always having occupied this sort of rung on the social ladder. How far the evidence supports this belief will become clearer as this book progresses, but, for the moment, let us assume it to be true and equate morris with village activity.)

Morris lives by the impact it makes in the moment: such events tend to be recorded at first hand, or not at all. It is therefore reasonable to suggest that the only morris events we know about are those which happened to be seen by somebody who was both literate and sufficiently interested to write them down. Unfortunately most people who were literate were not interested, and most people who were interested were not literate. Following this line of thought, we can draw a few hypothetical conclusions.

1) The writer would have been an outsider: someone from a different level of society noting down a visual scene without much feeling for the social context and purpose of the dance.
2) The writer's attention and interest were most likely to be caught by the unusual. (From which the historian is expected to reconstruct a balanced picture!)
3) Since the literate classes were unlikely to go out looking for the morris, we ought to expect the majority of reports to come from the (presumably) rare occasions when morris was brought into a literate environment: royal courts, courts of law, aristocratic houses and churches.

Add to this the thought that, while records may be well looked after in the libraries of the gentry or in government archives, they have a much harder time in damp and fire-prone, mouse-ridden cottages. Now we can begin to get some idea of how the cards are stacked against folk customs. The Fates allow us little more than the occasional glimpse of our ancestors – and then only through a filter of alien attitude.

This situation starts to improve round about 1800 when the Collectors of Curiosities begin to enter the field: Brand, Strutt, Hone and the editors of the *Gentleman's Magazine*. These men were still outsiders and their work may be seen as the collection, collation and publishing of reports and quotations, rather than first-hand observation, but they were genuinely interested, they were supremely literate, and their publications circulated widely. If we were to move on another hundred years we would find that political thought was beginning to see opportunities among the lower levels of society and that the 'working class' had become a legitimate subject for academic study. But 1900 lies beyond the range of this book.

There is one more facet of the written record that has put a slant onto our evidence for early morris. Of all human activities, the one that is most rigorously recorded and carefully preserved is the official management of money. Much of our history is extracted from account books, and morris follows the pattern. Thus, when the morris dancers were paid to appear before the lord, or for the church, we know about it; but when they danced in front of their friends and relatives for a collection of beer-money, we don't.

As a final and powerful demonstration of the gulf that separated village life from the world of the literate, here are two extracts from letters among the papers of the Verney family of Claydon House, Buckinghamshire.

22nd May 1716
We have Whitsun Ales all about us, which brings such abundance of rabble and the worst sort of company round us that I wish no mischiefs happen. Old Oliffe alarmed all the town on Sunday night crying out "Thieves!" and all the neighbours went to his assistance upon his letting off two guns; his daughter was come home to him without clothes, he sent her back again for them, and tis thought some of the King's companions did it to fright the old man. I can't help giving the Morrises money when they come, for they tell me everybody doing it is the best way to send them going.
26th May 1716
All the routs now as to the Whitsun Ales is over, it has cost two and a half guineas and half a crown in all, and yet I gave as little as anybody.
Lady Verney in *Verney Letters*, 1930.

* * * * *

The raw materials of the historian can be seen as passing through three processes: events are recorded; the records are preserved; and then these records are recovered and interpreted. My notes have already suggested how the recording and preservation processes are likely to have given shape to our picture of ancient morris; now I want to give a brief thought to the third phase, recovery. Recovery is seldom the work of one person: seldom a clear leap back to original source books. Rather, the collector in a library feels his way among the threads and clues left by others who have trodden a similar path and he leans, from time to time, on the transcriptions published by scholars who have studied the older manuscript documents. Every person connected with this process has left some mark upon the material, if only because they attract attention to the material they mention, and help perpetuate the obscurity of the material they omit. Collection cannot be separated from selection: and selection is a subjective process.

Honesty now directs that I should set down a few personal thoughts in order to give warning of the bias that I shall inevitably be putting upon the material.

For me, morris is for dancing. Faced with a written account of morris, the questions that rise first in my mind are:

'What were they doing?'

'What were they doing it for?'

'What else was going on around them?' (i.e. what sort of event were they taking part in?)

Questions that start with 'Why' I prefer to avoid, because they imply that we understand the motivation of the old dancers, and I approach with caution any modern writer who makes this claim. To ask 'Why' is to invite supposition: and if supposition is repeated often enough it grows to look very like fact.

My intention has been to gather together all the accounts of morris events that I could find; set them down in date order; and then take a long hard look to see what conclusions seem reasonable. The list contains a fair share of oddities (for reasons that we can now begin to understand) and it would be all too easy to hitch one's wagon to some of the more eccentric stories and come up with some very strange conclusions. I shall therefore attempt to avoid this trap by casting the net wide and leaving the laws of statistics to even out the eccentricity. The concept of 'event' is also worth emphasis because those accounts that identify time and place are safer guides to the truth than the sort of report that starts, 'My father used to say that forty years ago ...'. At the very outset one has to have a working definition in order to know what to gather and what to leave behind: mine was, and still is:

Morris is what the ordinary people of the time referred to as 'Morris'.

This definition becomes a little difficult to apply on the Continent, and in some English periods, when a variety of dances were commonly called morisco (or a name something like it). Here, my policy has been to include the dance in the survey where there is a reasonable possibility that it may have influenced (or become) English morris, but not otherwise.

A preliminary glance through the material has already suggested to me that the morris of the earliest records is fundamentally different from the morris we know today. This has prompted two questions.

1) How far back goes the sort of dance we now think of as morris?
2) Before that time, what sort of performance was represented by the words 'morris', 'morisco', 'mourisca', et cetera?

The break in the story that these questions imply may or may not exist, but they do seem to mark a useful direction from which to approach the subject.

Following the general pattern of these principles, I was led at first to omit references from works of fiction. Then after second thoughts I realised that certain facts can be gleaned even from fictional accounts.

Firstly, the author has heard about morris.

Secondly, the author expected readers to know what was meant by 'morris'.

Thirdly, any description was likely to have roots in the real world at the time of writing. (The author may have set the story in the past, but it is still the time of writing that is our safest guide.)

Consequently I have made use of fictional material where this has something interesting to offer.

'Why stop at 1850?' This is a question that arises quite naturally from the stated range of this book and deserves an answer before I wind up this section of personal reflections. I see 1850 (give or take a few years) as the start of the information explosion. If we add fifty-five or sixty years of living memory onto the front end of our present revival of interest in folk material, we get back to around 1850. Those who work their way backwards from the present, either studying dances, or studying the personalities and family relationships of the dancers, find they run out of information at about the same date. In several ways, therefore, morris information is different after 1850 from what it was before. There is a lot more of it, for one thing, and the detail is more reliable, for we are beginning to get reports from the dancers themselves. We also begin to see how morris follows different styles in the different regions of England. This improvement in the information supply has given rise to specialist studies which have recovered (and are still recovering) enormous amounts of detail. My object has been to review all the evidence for morris in a single volume and my only hope of achieving this aim is to draw a line at 1850.

Any history that follows a particular subject through time has some degree of unreality built into it, for events, as they happen, are part of a continuum of life, and when an historian chooses a single thread as centre-piece for his story then the balance must undergo some change. In the holidays of early nineteenth-century Lancashire, morris dancing played a significant part: so did badger baiting. It is a modern judgement reaching back into the past that decides morris dancing is worthy of study and revival, while badger baiting is not. I offer no solution to this problem. Indeed, I am not even sure that there is a problem: perhaps it is simply the price we pay for converting the tedium of archives into the fun of history.

CHAPTER 2

A HISTORY OF HISTORIES
A review of earlier work

A short excursion among the writings about morris will soon reveal that a substantial part is made up from quotations repeated from earlier writers. Time after time in book after book do we read Blount's definition of morisco; or see an engraving of the Betley window; or hear of a curious old tract concerning elderly dancers in Herefordshire. With great frequency are passages marked by a footnote such as 'Douce' or 'Brand'. In this multiple re-cycling of material it is easy to lose track of the historical context of an original statement and forget the character and purpose of its author, so in an attempt to bring the picture back into focus, I have prepared a Plain Man's Guide to the Written Sources.

This Guide is concerned with published material: material from authors who had something to say about morris and wanted other people to know. Sources of less deliberate character will not appear until Chapter 6. A few words of caution before I begin: these sketches are not intended to be gems of biographical research, neither are they comprehensive reviews. Their prime purpose is to give the reader an idea of *what sort* of publication we are dealing with, and then to pick out the bits that are important for our history. The sketches are set down in strict date order (using the date of first publication) so we can notice how opinions changed with time, and so we can distinguish influencer from the influenced. Qualification for inclusion in the Guide comes down to personal choice, but the thoughts that lie behind that choice can be listed:

1) Original sources that are frequently referred to by later writers.
2) People who give their ideas about what morris was like in their own day (provided their own day was before 1850).
3) People who give their ideas about the history of morris.
4) Important secondary sources; reference works that have harvested quotations and references about morris from a wide world of books and plays. Brand, Strutt and Hone provide such easy access to the material that they are often quoted as though they were primary sources.

* * * * *

1582 – Christopher Fetherston

If we recall that the common people couldn't write, and that those who could formed a stratum of society that had very little interest in the fun of the lower classes, then it should not surprise us too much when we find that the first literary reference to English morris is in the form of a complaint. In the London of 1582 there was published a booklet written by a Puritan, Christopher Fetherston, called (and one can almost hear him relishing the title) *A Dialogue agaynst light, lewde and lascivious dauncing.*

The dialogue is between Juvenis and a Minister, and in response to a question about the sort of dancing that went on at May Games, the Minister lets fly.

> For the abuses whiche are committed in your maygaymes are infinite. The first whereof is this, that you doe use to attyre men in womans apparrell, whom you doe most commenly call maymarrions, whereby you infringe that straight commaundement whiche is given in Deut. 22.5.[1] That men must not put on womens apparrell for feare of enormities. Nay, I myself have seene in a maygaime a troupe, the greater part wherof hath been men, and yet have they been attyred so like unto women, that theyr faces being hidde (as they were indeede) a man coulde not discerne them from women. What an horrible abuse was this? What abhominable sinnes might have hereupon ensued?
>
> The seconde abuse, which of all other is the greatest, is this, that it hath been toulde that your morice dauncers have daunced naked in nettes: what greater entisement unto naughtines could have been devised? The thirde abuse is, that you (because you will loose no tyme) doe use commonly to runne into woodes in the night time, amongst maidens, to fet bowes [fetch boughs], in so muche as I have hearde of tenne maidens whiche went to fet May, and nine of them came home with childe.

The idea of dancing naked in nets has never been satisfactorily explained, so the reader's imagination may wander over fish-net body-stockings, or some sort of cross between a hammock and a trampoline. If clues are wanted, there is the 'coranto danced on the ropes' in the Old Meg pamphlet of 1609, and a misericord at Worcester which shows a goat being mounted by a woman who appears naked except for a net cloak.

[1.] "The woman shall not wear that which pertaineth unto a man, neither shall a man put on a woman's garment: for all that do so are abomination unto the Lord thy God."

1583 – Phillip Stubbes

It is not uncommon for natural perversity to bend our efforts so that the end product bears little resemblance to our original intention. So it was with some puritan writings. Phillip Stubbes published his book *Anatomie of Abuses* in 1583 with the obvious intention of pulling down scorn and disgust upon the irreverent behaviour he described, but his efforts produced the best, the most colourful (and one suspects, the most accurate) account of early morris that has survived for our study. Indeed, such is the enthusiasm that shines through his words that one might be forgiven for questioning the purity of his puritanism. He does not use the word 'morris' but there seems little reason to doubt that his 'Lustie Guttes' performing the 'Devilles Daunce' would have been described as morris dancers by a contemporary of less dyspeptic character. Stubbes writes:

> Firste, all the wilde heades of the Parishe, couventyng together, chuse them a Graund Capitaine (of all mischeef) whome thei innoble with the title of my Lorde of Misserule, and hym thei croune with great solemnitie, and adopt for their kyng. This kyng anointed, chuseth for the twentie, fourtie, threescore, or a hundred lustie Guttes like to hymself, to waite uppon his Lordely majestie, and to guarde his noble persone. Then every one of these his menne, he investeth with his Liveries, of Greene, Yellowe, or some other light wanton colour. And as though that were not (baudie) gaudie enough I should saie, thei bedecke themselves with Scarffes, Ribons and Laces, hanged all over with golde Rynges, precious stones, and other Jewelles: this doen, thei tye about either legge twentie, or fourtie belles, with riche hande kercheefes in their handes, and somtymes laied a crosse over their shoulders and neckes, borrowed for the moste parte of their pretie Mopsies and loovyng Bessies, for bussyng them in the darcke. Thus all thynges settc in order, then have thei their Hobbie horses, Dragons and other Antiques, together with their baudie Pipers, and thunderyng Drommers, to strike up the Devilles Daunce withall, then marche these Heathen companie towardes the Churche and Churche yarde, their Pipers pipyng, their Drommers thonderyng, their stumppes Dauncyng, their belles iynglyng, their handkerchefes swyngyng about their heades like madmen, their Hobbie horses, and other monsters skirmishyng amongst the throng: and in this sorte thei goe to the Churche (though the Minister bee at Praier or Preachyng) dauncyng and swingyng their handercheefes over their heades, in the Churche, like Devilles incarnate, with suche a confused noise, that no manne can hearo his own voice. Then the foolishe people, thei looke, thei stare, thei laugh, thei fleere, and mounte upon formes and pewes, to see

these goodly pageauntes, solemnized in this sorte. Then after this, aboute the Churche thei goe againe and againe, and so forth into the Churche yarde, where thei have comonly their Sommer haules, their Bowers, Arbours, and banquettyng houses set up, wherein thei feaste, banquet, and daunce all that daie, and (peradventure) all that night too. And thus these terrestrial furies spend the Sabbaoth daie.

"Gold rings, precious stones and other jewels" suggest that the dancers were fairly well up the social ladder: not quite the labourers and artisans that were the backbone of nineteenth-century morris. The phrase, "goodly pageants", is strangely out of context: I take it to mean that the occasion started out as a proper church function (perhaps a Corpus Christi procession) and that it was only later taken over by the rowdy element.

From the antagonistic writings of Fetherston and Stubbes one message rings out loud and clear: among all the disgust with the fun, the colour, the sexual immorality and shock at the dancers' discourtesy toward the Church, there is not the slightest suggestion that morris might represent a rival ritual, or have serious pre-Christian connections (witchcraft or heresy, as it would then have been described). The sex is the ordinary, down-to-earth practical variety – no hint of a fertility ritual. What Puritan could have failed to use such cudgels – had they existed? Indeed, a more general reading of Puritan material leads me to suspect that they did not condemn all fun and dancing out of hand: they saw the devil in the dance only when it distracted the people from church services, or encouraged behaviour in direct conflict with Church teaching. A subtle, but I think an important, point.

1589 – Thoinot Arbeau

Jehan Tabourot (1520–1595) was a high-ranking churchman of distinguished family who lived in Langres, near Dijon in eastern France. He had a great affection for dances of all kinds and at the advanced age of sixty-nine he wrote his *Orchesography*, first published in 1589 under the anagrammatic pen-name of Thoinot Arbeau. This book, in the form of instructions to a pupil, sets down step notation, music and background notes for forty dances, one of which is morris (*morisque* in the French). This one dance is the only record we have of a morris, prior to the *Morris Book* of 1907, that gives sufficient information for the dance to be reconstituted into a performance – but unfortunately it comprises no more than a tune and a tapping of the heels: clearly it is a poor remnant of an earlier dance. Arbeau paints a brief picture of a morris presentation: –

In fashionable society when I was young [say about 1540] a small boy, his face daubed with black and his forehead swathed in a white or yellow kerchief, would make an appearance after supper. He wore leggings covered with little bells and performed a morris, wherein he advanced the length of the room, made a kind of passage and then moving backwards retraced his steps to the place from whence he had started. Then he executed a new passage and he continued thus making various passages which delighted the spectators.
Lady Evans' translation from the French, 1948.

The remark that he puts into the mouth of his pupil, "I will teach them to my lackey," confirms Arbeau's view that the scene described above shows morris dance in its proper social position. Arbeau adds, "Originally they [morris dances] were executed by striking the feet together, but because the dancers found this too painful, they tried striking the heels only while keeping the toes rigid." This striking of the feet together caused gout and Arbeau believed this was the reason for morris falling into disuse.

It is an interesting sidelight to note that the *Orchesography* was quite close in time to the production of the *Balet Comique de la Royne* (1581), an event which is widely considered to be the progenitor of classical ballet. The world of dance was certainly beginning to grow and diversify.

1598 – John Stow

The historian and antiquary, John Stow, published *A Survay of London* in 1598 when he was 73 years old. Although his book contains no details of the morris dance itself, it does give us a useful picture of some of the events in which morris dancers made an appearance. These events fall into two groups: Mayings, and Marching Watches. Stow describes the Mayings thus:

I find also that in the moneth of May, the Citizens of London, of all estates, lightlie in every parish, or sometimes two or three parishes joyning together, had their several mayinges, and did fetch in Maypoles, with divers warlike shewes, with good Archers, Morrice daunccers, and other devises for pastime all the day long, and towardes the evening they had stage playes and bonfires in the streetes...

It is perhaps worth noticing at this early date that the pastime was morris dancers – not morris dancing – in other words the dance was a display before an audience. Elsewhere he adds: "These greate Mayinges and Maygames ... with the triumphant setting up of the greate shafte [at the church of St Andrew, called Undershaft] ... have not beene so freely used as afore." And the reason he gives for this decline is the riot, or "insurrection of youthes against Alianes on Mayday, 1517". These youths were apprentices who took exception to the way foreigners resident in London were given advantages over the native Londoners.

In addition to a standing watch, which we can think of as the constabulary, there was also a marching watch which processed through the City twice a year on the vigils of St John the Baptist, and of St Peter and St Paul the Apostles (23rd and 28th of June). Stow mentions two thousand men as taking part and his list of old soldiers, gunners, archers, pikemen, et cetera, suggests that the prime purpose was a display of military strength, although "divers pageantes", including morris dancers, seem to have become attached. "For where the Mayor had besides his Giant three Pageants, each of the Shiriffes had besides their Giantes but two Pageants each [with] their Morris Dance, and one henchman ...."

These marching watches had continued from 'time out of mind' up until the year 1539, when fifteen thousand took part and it seems King Henry thought that costs had got out of hand, so the processions lapsed. There were several attempts at revival, but they had no lasting success.

1600 – Kemp's Jig

A company of London players called the Lord Chamberlain's Men included among their number Richard Burbage, William Shakespeare and a very popular comedian, William Kemp. Now Kemp had a keen eye for publicity and so, when he walked out of the company in 1599 amid general ill-feeling, he judged it was time for a bit of personal advertising – he would dance a morris jig from London to Norwich. It took him twenty-seven days to accomplish this enterprise: nine and a bit days spent dancing his journey, interspersed with eighteen rest days. The story was told in print and Will's shrewd eye for a title called it *Kemp's Nine Daies' Wonder* and gave us a phrase that is still in common use. The woodcut on the title page of this booklet is the earliest illustration we have that is unequivocally identified as a morris dancer.

Publicity was obviously the prime concern in this adventure and the winning of wagers also played a part, so one can see why Cecil Sharp dismissed the event as a "somewhat ridiculous and very un-Morris-like escapade". Nevertheless, it should be remembered that Kemp was a famous actor with a speciality in clown's and fool's parts, so for this reason alone one might expect him to know about morris. (Why else should he have chosen to perform a morris jig?) If there are any doubts on this point then one may be sure that the hundreds of people who came out to watch, particularly those who had staked money, would have been vociferous in

LONDON

their objections and disruptive, had he not been dancing the 'morrice' as he claimed. (However, we ought to remind ourselves that we have no second witness. All our information comes from the pen of Will Kemp himself.)

Some fourteen years before, in 1586, he had been a member of a dancing troupe visiting Denmark and it is recorded that "Kemp, particularly, impressed the Danes with his famous Morris Dance" (see Woodward, *Ballet*, 1977). There can be little question therefore that William Kemp was a very competent performer of *what was then known as morris*. Sharp's remark clearly sprang from his own conviction that morris was little affected by the passing years; he thus expected the morris style of Queen Elizabeth's day to be closely similar to the performances that he himself had seen. Few people today would hold this view quite so strongly.

Forward I went with my hey de gaies to Ilford.
Or again
.... and to our jumps we fell.

These are about the only clues we get as to the nature of the dance Kemp used for his progress and they give us very little idea about what he was actually doing. Some of the time he was travelling fairly fast and this argues a dance that was simple.

> I set on towards Thetford, dauncing that tenne mile in three houres.

At other times the way was foul and ill-marked which, again, suggests a simplicity of dance. It is clear enough that a lot of energy was required and there are hints that the dance may have been used as an endurance test to settle challenges along the road, and no doubt boost the takings. (Graham alludes to a similar competitive feature in nineteenth-century Lancashire[1].)

On a couple of occasions a girl joined Kemp in his morris, each being fitted with bells before dancing (this seems to have been important). The young girl from Chelmsford insisted on "the olde fashion with napking on her armes" and this points to a similarity with the open sleeves that hang from the shoulders in the woodcut. The other "lusty Country lasse" Kemp refers to as his "merry Mayde-marrian".

This event, commonly called 'Kemp's Jig', reminds us that in Elizabethan days the word 'jig' carried some sense of a complete presentation, not just a single dance. The modern colloquial phrase 'doing a gig' is a return to something quite close to the earlier meaning.

1609 – Old Meg of Herefordshire

An anonymous ten-page pamphlet was printed in 1609 bearing the awkward title of *Old Meg of Hereford-shire, for a Mayd-Marian: and Hereford Towne for a Morris-daunce. Or Twelve Morris-Dancers in Hereford-shire, of twelve hundred yeares old*. It was marked to be sold from "The great South doore of Paules" in London and it recounted how a horse-race near Hereford was to have been enlivened by the introduction of a hobby-horse, but that the hobby-horse arrived as part of a complete team of morris dancers, and that these morris dancers were of quite remarkable age.

> Lords went a Maying, the wombe of the spring being great with child of pleasure

The unrestrained enthusiasm and ebullience of the author suggest that little things like factual accuracy were unlikely to trouble him, and the dominant theme, that every participant in the morris was close to or over one hundred years of age, is another signal for caution in any interpretation.

[1] *Lancashire and Cheshire Morris Dances*, 1911. An old dancer remembered being challenged once on the roadside when he was driving. He accepted, and kept up the jig longer than it was wanted. A bystander said, "You have danced down the best dancer in Oldham town".

By way of illustrating the style, here is part of his introduction to Old Hall, one of the musicians.

.... thou givest the men light hearts by thy Pype, and the women light heeles by thy Taber: O wonderfull Pyper, O admirable Taber-man, make use of thy worth, even after death, that art so famously worthy in thy life, both for thy age, skill, & thy unbruized Taber, who these three-score yeares has kept her maydenhead sound and uncrackt, and neither lost her first voyce, or her fashion: once for the Countryes pleasure imitate that Bohemian Zisca, who at his death gave his Souldiers a strict commaund, to flea his skin off, and cover a Drum with it, that alive & dead, he might sound like a terror in the eares of his enemies: so thou sweete Hereford Hall, bequeath in thy last will, thy Velom-spotted skin, to cover Tabors: at the sound of which, to set all the shires a dauncing.

There were two musicians, one with a 'Trebble Violim' and Old Hall with his pipe and tabor, four whifflers with staves to clear the way and twelve dancers: it is interesting that the hobby-horse and Maid Marian are both numbered among the dancers. Maid Marian, old Meg Goodwin of Erdistand, is said to have been threescore years a maid and twenty years otherwise, at the age of one hundred and twenty. The costumes are described as follows:

The musicians and the twelve dancers, had long coats of the old fashion, high sleeves gathered at the elbows, and hanging sleeves behind: the stuff red buffin, striped with white, girdles with white, stockings white, and red roses to their shoes: the one six, a white jews cap with a jewel, and a long red feather: the other a scarlet jews cap, with a jewel and a white feather: so the hobby-horse, and so the maid-marian was attired in colours: the whifflers had long staves, white and red.

Another quotation is interesting for the links it offers between the morris jig, the galliard and the 'jig' performed on stage after the end of a play, by way of rounding off a performance. It may also be a contemporary dig at Shakespeare. "Kemp's Morris to Norwich was no more to this than a galliard, on a common stage, at the end of an old dead Comedy, is to a coranto danced on the ropes."

1623 – William Shakespeare

In the works of Shakespeare there are but three brief passages with direct reference to morris dancing – scarcely sufficient material to warrant inclusion in this particular chapter, were it not for the extra magic that the name Shakespeare lends to any reference.

King Henry VI, Part 2, Act III, Scene 1 (written in the period 1584–1592). The Duke of York says of the rebel John Cade, he "fought so long till that his thighs with darts were almost like a sharp-quill'd porpentine; and in the end being rescu'd, I have seen him caper upright like a wild Morisco, shaking the bloody darts as he his bells."

Here the word *morisco* clearly attaches to the person rather than the dance.

King Henry V, Act II, Scene 4 (written in the period 1594–1599). The Dauphin, speaking to his father the King of France about strengthening their defences, says: "'Tis meet we all go forth to view the sick and feeble parts of France; and let us do it with no show of fear – no, with no more than if we heard that England were busied with a Whitsun morris-dance."

Morris-dance is here used for a symbol of a country in political tranquillity.

All's Well That Ends Well, Act II, Scene 2. (written in the period 1599–1608). In some banter between the Countess and a Clown the theme runs: "I have an answer will serve all men." ".... Will your answer serve fit to all questions?" "As fit as .... as a pancake for Shrove Tuesday, a morris for Mayday, ..."

1656 and 1679 – Thomas Blount

In a dictionary called *Glossographia* (1656), Blount gives: "Morisco (Span.) a Moor; also a Dance so called, wherein there were usually five men, and a Boy dressed in a Girles habit, whom they call the Maid Marrian, or perhaps Morian, from the Ital. Morione a Head-peece, because her head was wont to be gaily trimmed up. The common people call it a Morris Dance."

Thomas Blount was a barrister with an interest in village customs and in oddities gathered from tenancy agreements. In 1679 he published his *Fragmenta Antiquitatis; or Antient Tenures of Land and Jocular Customs of some Manors* which included the following entry:

KIDLINGTON At Kidlington in Oxfordshire, the Custom is, that on Monday after Whitson-Week, there is a fat live Lamb provided, and the Maids of the Town, having their Thumbs tied behind them, run after it, and she that with her Mouth takes and holds the Lamb, is declared 'Lady of the Lamb', which being dressed, with the Skin hanging on, is carried on a long Pole before the Lady and her Companions to the Green, attended with Music, and a Morisco Dance of Men, and another of Women, where the Rest of the Day is spent in Dancing, Mirth and merry Glee. The next Day the Lamb is part baked, boiled, and roast, for the Lady's Feast, where she sits majestically, at the upper End of the Table, and her Companions with her, with Music and other Attendants, which ends the Solemnity.

Although this passage is often quoted in discussions on morris, in particular by advocates of women's morris, it is clear that the morris was a comparatively minor element in this colourful village festival. Later records make no further mention of morris at Kidlington – but however, four miles away at Kirtlington we do hear of morris danced at Lamb Ales (up until 1858, if we don't count the recent revival). Several writers, led by Thomas Hearne (1723), have claimed a mistake by Blount and I think they are probably right – Kirtlington is the place.

1740 – Francis Peck

The sounds and seas with all their finnie drove
Now to the moon in wav'ring morrice move.

So wrote Milton in his *Comus* in 1634. Francis Peck, who published a substantial study of the life and works of Mr John Milton in 1740, made this quotation his excuse for offering some supplementary information on the morris dance.

The morris or moorish dance was first brought into England, as I take it, in Edward III time, when John of Gaunt returned from Spain, where he had been to assist his father-in-law, Peter, K. of Castile, against Henry the bastard. This dance was usually performed abroad by an equal number of young men, who danced in their shirts with ribands and little bells about their legs. But here in England they have always an odd person besides, being a boy dressed in a girl's habit, whom they called Maid Marian. The place where they danced was often in the field, and called the five, seven, or nine, men's morris, just according to the number of the dancers. ... I cannot forbear observing on the boy dressed in girl's cloaths introduced into this dance, that, tho' the young folks of England had, by this Spanish expedition, got a new diversion, yet they could not forbear dashing it with their old favorit one of Maid Marian.

The 'boy dressed in a girl's habit' is a phrase in common with Blount's *Glossographia,* but there is a curious discrepancy in the numbers of dancers: Blount has five men and the boy, whereas Peck has 'an equal number of young men' (presumably meaning an even number) plus the boy. There was an outdoor game called Nine Men's Morris which had been popular in Elizabethan times: it was commonly played with pieces on a 'board' made of holes cut into the grass. There was no connection at all between the game and morris dancing, but it looks as though Peck was in some confusion on the point and adjusted his numbers to suit this particular red herring. It is worth emphasis that Peck believed morris dancing and Maid Marian to be separate customs that came together in England.

1743 – Franz Junius

When mention is made of morris dancers blacking their faces, there is often reference to a Latin quotation from Junius. Franz Junius lived from 1589 to 1677 and the quotation comes from his *Etymologicum Anglicanum,* published posthumously in 1743. Put into English, the quotation runs:

> They generally smear their faces with soot and wear a foreign style of dress to take part in such spectacles so as to appear to be Moors, or so that people think that they have flown some considerable distance from a distant country and brought with them a strange type of recreation.
> Translation by Mark West, 1983.

1755 – Dr Samuel Johnson

In his magnificent *Dictionary of the English Language* the following entries occur.

To Dance – To move in measure; to move with steps correspondant to the sound of instruments.

Morris/Morris-Dance (that is moorish or morisco-dance)
1. A dance in which bells are gingled, or staves or swords clashed, which was learned by the Moors, and was probably a kind of Pyrrhick or military dance.
2. Nine mens Morris. A kind of play with nine holes in the ground.

Morris-Dancer – One who dances a la moresco, the moorish dance. "There went about the countrey a set of morrice-dancers, composed of ten men, who danced a maid marian and a tabor and pipe." (Temple)

The quotation comes from Sir William Temple, writing about a pamphlet in the library of the Earl of Leicester, in his *Essay upon Health and Long Life* (1701). It is clear that the Earl's pamphlet was *Old Meg of Herefordshire.*

1762 – Giovanni Gallini

Signor Gallini was Director of the dances at the Royal Theatre in the Haymarket and in 1762 he published *A Treatise on the Art of Dancing* in which he cautiously approaches morris.

> I do not know whether I shall not stand in need of an apology for mentioning here a dance once popular in England, but to which the idea of low is now currently annexed. It was originally adapted from the Moors, and is still known by the name of Morris-dancing, or Moresc-dance. It is danced with swords, by persons oddly disguised, with a great deal of antic rural merriment: it is true that this diversion is now almost exploded, being entirely confined to the lower classes of life, and only kept up in some counties.

He expresses a belief that the dance may once have been current among the higher ranks of society before descending to its present low level and he hopefully adds that the dance is "susceptible enough of improvement, to rescue it from the contempt it may have incurred through its being chiefly in use among the vulgar... Rude, as it was, it might require refinement, but it did not, perhaps, deserve to become quite obsolete."

1776 – Sir John Hawkins

In 1776 Sir John Hawkins published *A General History of Music* in five volumes, which included two paragraphs about morris. Sir John thought it highly probable that the morris dance was introduced into this and other countries in the century preceding Henry VIII and he goes on: "It is indisputable that this dance was the invention of the Moors, for to dance a Morisco is a term that occurs in some of our old English writers." [He probably means Blount.] Here the emphasis seems too heavy for the context and one wonders whether people were beginning to question this origin. He further clarifies his point by describing the dance as one of the recreations of the Moors in Spain.

Sir John describes the contemporary morris dance thus:

> There are few country places in this kingdom where it is not known; it is a dance of young men in their shirts, with bells at their feet, and ribbands of various colours tied round their arms, and flung across their shoulders. Some writers, Shakespear in particular, mention a Hobby-horse and a Maid Marian, as necessary in this recreation.

[Untrue of Shakespeare – he was probably thinking of *Old Meg of Herefordshire* as quoted in Sir William Temple's Essay, while his 'young men in their shirts' is an echo from Peck.]

1777 – John Brand
Back in 1725 Henry Bourne had published a collection of curiosities with the title *Antiquitates Vulgares* – for example:

> There is another custom observed at this time [New Year], which is called among us mumming which is a changing of clothes between men and women, who then dressed in each others habits go from one neighbours house to another and partake of their Christmas cheer.

John Brand, a rector of two London churches, re-published Bourne's material in 1777 together with substantial additions of his own under the title *Observations on Popular Antiquities*. This work went through a number of editions, with Henry Ellis taking over control from Brand in 1813 and being followed by Hazlitt in 1849. The final edition came in 1905, by which time the title had become *Faiths and Folklore*. Sprinkled through the pages of the eight editions there are multitudes of factual and literary references to morris, to sword dancing, and to related customs.

1778 – George Tollet
George Tollet (1725–1779) was a barrister who led a secluded life devoted to his books in Betley Hall, not far from Crewe. This house, which probably dated from 1621, contained a painted glass window of unknown origin, but which was widely supposed to represent figures from the May Game or Morris. The window led George Tollet to write a dissertation under the title, *Mr Tollet's Opinion concerning the Morris Dancers upon his Window*, which was then inserted, for no very obvious reason, into an edition of the plays of Shakespeare by Samuel Johnson and George Steevens published in 1778. The *Opinion* is principally concerned with giving a detailed description of the figures, but Mr Tollet also reflects upon early references to May Games and morris:–

> A story attributed to Chaucer of the Court emerging on a May-day morn to gather flowers and foliage [This story comes from *The Court of Love*, a poem included among early collections of Chaucer's work but now known to be spurious and dating from around 1500.]:–
> A similar account from the time of Henry VIII:–
> Holinshed's report (1577) of summer kings and queens with sport and

dancing about maypoles before 1306 [This is almost certainly 1577 decoration added to the 1306 story.]:–
Francis Peck's conjectures about the arrival of morris in England in the middle 1300s.

Tollet develops Peck's idea of morris meeting up with Maid Marion and supposes that these imported morris or moorish dances were soon added on to the celebration of May-day, which he describes as "a very ancient custom". He quotes Stow's *Survay of London* where the May pastimes included morris dancers.

"We are authorised," writes Tollet, "by the poets Ben Jonson and Drayton, to call some of the representations on my window Morris Dancers", although he goes on to express surprise at the absence of Moorish black faces, swords, staves and ribboned shirts. Brass bells about the knees are there, but these are common among the northern nations according to Olaus Magnus.[1] Perhaps, he suggests, the window represents performers in the May Game before the arrival of the morris dance. Certainly the maypole on the window carries the message, 'A Mery May'.

His final paragraph runs: "Such are my conjectures upon a subject of much obscurity; but it is high time to resign it to one more conversant with the history of our ancient dresses."

Notwithstanding a lot of careful detective work (see E.J. Nicol, *JEFDSS*, December 1953) there is still some uncertainty about the date of the Betley window. A recent discussion with the Victoria and Albert Museum, where the window is now housed, suggests the following as most probable. The material elements of the window, the colours in particular, point to the early seventeenth century, and the date of 1621, noted by Tollet over a door at Betley, is quite plausible as the date when the window was made. The figures were presumably copied from an earlier source, for the style of dress can be dated to 1505 plus or minus fifteen years. A close similarity between some of the Betley figures and those in a van Meckenem engraving of about 1495 has often been recognised.

1790 – *Gentleman's Magazine*

This monthly periodical was started in 1731 by Edward Cave who edited it under the pseudonym of Sylvanus Urban. Its main purpose in the early days was to publish reports of Parliamentary debates, in spite of the fact that this was against the law at the time, and it went on to carry comment and readers' letters on current affairs, arts, antiquities and customs. The letters, in particular, have provided some important early references to

---

[1.] Archbishop of Uppsala, writing c. 1555.

morris, and the date given here, 1790, marks the earliest one I have found – a letter describing Furry Day at Helston in Cornwall (see Chapter 6).

1801 – Joseph Strutt

Joseph Strutt was an engraver, a painter and a great reader who had published in 1801, shortly before his death, his best-known work, *Glig-Gamena Angel-Deod or, The Sports and Pastimes of the People of England*. (The Anglo-Saxon title was to be dropped from later editions.) This book was one of the first to take as its main subject the activities of common people, and the newness of the path obliged Strutt to gather his material from a study of original sources: not for him the comparatively easy task of chasing up references already located by somebody else. His book exhibits an order and a purpose which take it beyond the earlier Collections of Curiosities and make his work a pioneer step towards a study of social history. In parallel with Brand's *Popular Antiquities*, *Sports and Pastimes* ran through a series of editions and reprints throughout the whole of the nineteenth century (with the last edition of 1903 being reprinted in 1969).

Morris had long been accepted as an anglicised form of the word 'morisco' and so, without further thought, the dance was assumed to have Moorish origins. Strutt was the first writer to question this established view and he put forward his own opinion that the morris-dance originated from the fool's dance: the fool's dance being an ancient dance that had originally formed a part of the pageant belonging to the Festival of Fools. He believed that:

> The Morisco or Moor dance is exceedingly different from the morris-dance formerly practised in this country; it being performed with the castanets or rattles at the ends of the fingers and not with bells attached to various parts of the dress.
> (Note the word 'formerly' – morris is, as always, a dying art.)

The Festival of Fools was a mediaeval custom of ordinary people held around Christmas time and sometimes called the December Liberties. The theme was revolt against authority – a kicking over of traces – and since most mediaeval authority came from the Church, the Church was the main target. A 'Bishop' or 'Pope' of Fools was elected who would then deliver "lewd and vulgar discourses accompanied by actions equally reprehensible" (Hone).

In spite of Strutt's assertion that a direct link connected the fool's dance back to the Festival of Fools, the evidence, such as it is, paints a slightly different picture, with a fool's dance being more likely in a court entertainment than on the streets with the 'Bishop'. My feeling is that the name 'Fool's Dance' came to be applied to two different sorts of presentation, although one could of course postulate a third (unrecorded) street version.

1) A group of 'fools' (commonly five) dance around a young woman, competing for her favour. The 'favour' is a physical object, apple or ring, which led Barbara Lowe to describe the performance as Ring Morris. (There is no connection whatsoever with a modern style of morris once favoured by The Morris Ring and disrespectfully called 'Ring Morris'.)
2) A group of 'fools' (commonly three) equipped with swords and sometimes shields who dance around in a mock combat with the emphasis on dramatic movement and clashings. This sort of performance is also called the matachins.

Strutt also draws attention to the part played in Mayday customs by milkmaids, chimney sweeps and their Green Man. Recent thinking is beginning to suggest that links between this sort of custom and morris dancing may be closer than was thought a few years ago.

1807 – Francis Douce

Francis Douce was an educated gentleman from the time of George III with a wide-ranging interest, a lively curiosity and a strong collector's instinct – but always with an emphasis on the written word. To study a subject was to read what others had written about it and, perhaps, draw some conclusions. Getting up and going out to look for oneself was an idea yet to come, for travelling was still difficult, dangerous and expensive. In 1807 Douce published his *Illustrations of Shakespeare and of Ancient Manners*, a discussion of some of the details raised within the plays, and at the end of this work he included 'A Dissertation on the Ancient English Morris Dance'. (This link by association between Shakespeare and the morris is an interesting parallel to George Tollet's work, and there are several other cases of authors who got side-tracked into morris when their declared subject was Shakespeare.)

Some have sought the origin of the morris in the Pyrrhica saltatio of the ancients, a military dance which seems to have been invented by the Greeks, and was afterwards adopted by the Salii or priests of Mars. This continued to be practised for many ages, till it became corrupted by figures and gesticulations foreign to its original purpose. Such a dance was that well known in France and Italy by the name of the dance of fools or Matachins, who were habited in short jackets with gilt-paper helmets, long streamers tied to their shoulders, and bells to their legs. They carried in their hands a sword and buckler, with which they made a clashing noise, and performed various quick and sprightly evolutions.

This might be described as the 'classical' theory of morris origins and probably takes its flavour from a belief strongly held in those days, that anything worthwhile must have had origins in either Greece or Rome. However, Mr Douce does not offer this theory with any great personal conviction, neither does he endorse Peck's supposition of direct import from Spain, although he is inclined to accept that the remotest origins of the dance may well have been with the Moors. Instead, he offers a new thought: "It is much more probable that we had it [morris dance] from our Gallic neighbours, or even from the Flemings". This opinion seems to take its support from Arbeau's book, from three brief mentions in fifteenth-century France, and from a Flemish engraving by van Meckenem.

Douce's style makes it a little tricky to decide which of the many ideas he puts forward are the ones that carry his own personal endorsement. But if I understand him rightly, he would hang the development of morris on three pegs.

1) Pyrrhic dance: a Greek (or imitation of Greek) display dance on a military combat theme.
2) Moorish dance: a Spanish dance that has survived into the present (1807) as the fandango. Something of this dance may have dispersed across Europe, changing as it went, and scattered elements from this process may then have been gathered up to form peg number three.
3) English morris: of uncertain but possibly Gallic or Flemish origin.

The 'Wild Moriscos' (which originate in a faulty reading of Shakespeare) may be, he suggests, a mixture of the Pyrrhic and the Moorish strains of the dance. He goes on to note that the English records show morris to have been attendant upon a wide variety of different festivals and ceremonies. Also, the morris that accompanied Robin Hood at the May Games was substantially different from the simple morris of village couples around a maypole. He contradicts an opinion published by Joseph Ritson (*Robin Hood*, 1795) by making an important statement that was unfortunately missed by the Oxford Dictionary. "It is by no means clear that at any time Robin Hood and his companions were constituent characters in the morris." Indeed, Douce's extensive study of records and literary references to May Games and the morris pushed him to declare: "Wherever we turn, nothing but irregularity presents itself."

1827 and 1832 – William Hone

William Hone (1780–1842) was a writer, publisher and bookseller with a vast knowledge of antiquarian writings. Folklore, folk customs and the early history of the Church were among his particular interests and from his extensive reading he gathered together items that caught his fancy, added in letters from his wide circle of correspondents, and published the resulting miscellany as *The Every-Day Book* (1827) and *The Year Book* (1832). Many of the earlier writings about morris are extensively quoted by Hone and mixed in with information on other associated customs.

1890 – Sir James Frazer

Sir James Frazer wrote nothing about morris, but he did plant a powerful idea in the public imagination that has influenced many others who did. Sir James' amazingly successful book, *The Golden Bough* (first published 1890), starts from an enquiry into the rule of succession to the priesthood of Diana at Aricia and goes on to develop the idea of king sacrifice. The king is the figurehead and carries, in essence, the community's health, vigour and success. Whenever the powers of the king show signs of waning, then it is the duty of his people to kill him and find a replacement. As time goes by, this idea is subjected to modification so that an expendable person can be brought in as a king-substitute: this man is then treated like the king for a few days before being killed in vicarious sacrifice.

   This idea found fertile and receptive soil in the minds of Victorian people, where it filtered into the subconscious and even down to the levels of race memory, where it acquired instant antiquity. The public of the time seem to have had an enormous appetite for this sort of thing and *The Golden Bough* could be looked upon as voluminous evidence entered in support of an idea that had first been put into print by Sir Edward Tylor in 1871. Writing on primitive culture, Sir Edward had claimed that many of the actions and customs of the peasantry were survivals from the myths and ritual of a dimly seen, but somehow unifying, past.

1891 – Alfred Burton

There was an ancient and widespread custom of bringing in rushes to strew upon the floor of the church in order to provide some sort of insulation between cold feet and a colder floor. As with most other things, the nineteenth century brought a succession of changes to this custom. To start with, in the early days, there were changes of social attitude that found loose rushes no longer acceptable as a floor covering, so rushes ceased to be spread. But folk customs sometimes seem to flourish more strongly after their purpose has been pruned away and rushes continued to be brought to church for another fifty years and more. The cotton industry took root on the rising ground around Manchester and villages grew and coalesced into towns until the remaining wet places where rushes grew were a long way from the church. So rushes were loaded onto carts and the rushbearing custom became a rushcart procession. The style of morris dancing that had its centre in south-east Lancashire (now commonly called Northwest morris) was usually associated with rushcarts. The rushbearing custom provided the central feature in a week-long holiday that was originally timed to mark the end of harvest: the holiday itself being commonly called either a 'rushbearing' or a 'wakes'. The word 'wake' has its origin with the idea of keeping a-wake at a vigil to commemorate church dedication, and Dedication Day has always been a popular choice for the holding of a village festival. As the nineteenth century progressed there was a decreasing tolerance for the fighting and heavy drinking that had become dominant features in Wakes Week and slowly but surely the temperance fighters won the day. The taming of Wakes Week took the drive out of the rushcart procession and with it faded the morris dance.

When Alfred Burton wrote his book, *Rush-Bearing* (published 1891), active rushbearing and rushcart customs were a rarity and, like so many studies of folk material, his book was inspired by a wish to record what was left of a custom before the memory faded completely away. Morris dancing took a small but significant part in the rushcart processions and so the dance has a chapter to itself in his book: a chapter which contains a large and by now familiar collection of quotations with a few reminiscences of morris at wakes and rushbearings earlier in the century. The present-day view that Northwest morris is essentially different from morris in other parts of England did not enter Burton's thoughts and so we get no guidance at all on a couple of questions we would like to ask. Are the Northwest and the Cotswold morrises two shoots from the same stock? If so, when did the division occur?

1895 – Lilly Grove

Three general histories of dance have come my way which contain some reference to morris. That by Reginald St Johnston (1906) may be put aside as being too fanciful to assist in this present enquiry and so we are left with the works of Grove and Sachs. Mrs Grove (who was married to Sir James Frazer) wrote a volume titled simply, *Dancing* (published 1895, within a series called *The Badminton Library of Sports and Pastimes*), and this book is still perhaps the best balanced view of morris set within the context of all other dance. A close interest in morris tends to make one forget the world outside, and more than that, one comes to forget how suspect are the definitions we use to divide the world of dance into 'morris' and 'not-morris'. Mrs Grove's work does a lot to restore the perspective.

If I may digress for a moment into the world of archaeology: early in the twentieth century much interest was shown in the chipped stone tools of the Old Stone Age. These were collected with enthusiasm and the find-spots recorded on maps. After a few years the maps started to show an interesting distribution of these find-spots, suggesting centres of Old Stone Age occupation. It took a surprisingly long period of learned discussion before the penny dropped: what the maps really showed was where the collectors lived! This lesson needs to be remembered by all who work with collected dance material, and a thoughtful reading of Lilly Grove shows how our present knowledge is made up of spots of light scattered through geography and history that mark the presence of someone with the interest and ability to record a dance. The spots are often few, and the intervening blackness impenetrable, so any attempt to see links of style or purpose between the spots should be presented with caution and with modesty.

1907 – Cecil Sharp

Cecil Sharp (1859–1924) was a superb collector of music, song and dance. He was also an effective organiser and an inspiring leader. A group of devoted followers gathered about him and from this nucleus sprang a folk dance club (1910) which grew into the English Folk Dance Society (1911), which then combined with the Folk Song Society (1932) to form the English Folk Dance and Song Society – which is still very much Cecil Sharp's Society, even today, nearly eighty years after his death. It can be no more than speculation to wonder what morris would be like today if there had been no Cecil Sharp, for we cannot tell who may have grown to fill the void, but it is reasonable to suppose that morris would be far less widespread and that its stock of traditional dances would be cut by half. It could even be argued that without Sharp, morris might by now be finally extinct. These matters that have made Sharp the dominant name in English Folk over the last ninety years do not properly come within the range of this book. However, Sharp's views on the history of morris do; and here he was far less sound.

"We claim for this sketch no completeness": so starts the historical section of Sharp's first published work on morris (*Morris Book* Part I, 1907), while on the same page he goes on, "all that is to be gleaned of it [morris] from books consists only in scraps of information, most of them very brief, some contradictory; as a rule almost casually introduced in works upon dancing, ancient games and customs, and such like". It was a very fair appraisal of the situation seen in 1907. Sharp was inclined to accept his reading of Douce's view, that the morris dance was of Moorish origin, although much altered since its import, and he listed three arguments in support.

1) The derivation of the word 'morris' from 'morisco'. [Few people would dispute this, but it does not necessarily follow that the dance 'morris' derives from a dance called 'morisco'.]

2) The similarity between morris and the dances found on both sides of the Franco–Spanish border. [There is no doubt that some Basque dances are surprisingly similar to Cotswold morris, the only major difference between them being a quality of balletic athleticism on the part of the Basques. Whether the one influenced the other, and in which direction; whether both were influenced by the same external force which may, by now, have sunk without trace; whether we see a coincidental development along parallel but unconnected lines we cannot say with any confidence, for history provides no evidence.]

3) The custom of blacking faces among some English morris dancers. [The question of blackface looms large in many discussions of morris origins, but it is in fact a fairly rare occurrence if one looks at the whole range of traditional morris as collected. The only area in which it attains significant proportions is the Border morris of Shropshire, Hereford and Worcestershire and this poorly recorded tradition seems to have gathered up tambourines, triangles and bones from the 'nigger minstrel' shows that reached a peak of popularity towards the end of the nineteenth century. So how long had they had black faces? We don't know.]

One does not get very far when reading the Introductions in the various parts and editions of the *Morris Book* before realising that Cecil Sharp had an unquestioning conviction that traditional dance did not change. Phrases like, "Ancient and uninterrupted tradition" and "The purity of the tradition" help to create a picture of morris that stretches back through history like "Blackpool" through the rock. We have already seen how Kemp's Jig failed to fit in with Sharp's expectation and so earned a dismissive comment.

Rather more sinister is Sharp's reference to the account of morris given by Arbeau, for Sharp says, "This shows as nearly as possible the steps of the Morris as we have seen it danced in England today". He goes on to claim close similarity between the performance of Arbeau's little boy and a jig he had recently seen performed by William Kimber. Bearing in mind that Arbeau's description of the steps for morris runs like this:

> Tap right heel
> Tap left heel
> Tap right heel
> Tap left heel
> Tap heels
> Pause
>> Repeat

it is difficult to escape from the conclusion that Sharp was deluding himself into seeing what his convictions led him to expect. A serious fault in a collector. A slight excuse might be entered on Sharp's behalf over this particular incident: he may well have set off on the wrong tack after hearing Arbeau's tune played for the Bidford morris – an example of persistence and continuity, he called it – without realising that the tune had been lifted straight from Arbeau's book by the pageant master D'Arcy Ferris, when he formed the Bidford morris side twenty years before.

By the time the second edition of the *Morris Book* Part I was published in 1912, Cecil Sharp had gained a much wider knowledge of traditional dance in general, and in particular he had met the sword dances of northern England. This led him to believe that morris was very widely distributed, "pretty nearly all over Europe", and he noted that, "Morris is nearly always associated with certain strange customs which are apparently quite independent of the dance itself". By a chain of reasoning that is not altogether clear he deduces that "the Morris dance is a development of a pan-European, or even more widely extended custom". He concludes this part of his introduction with the highly significant statement: "The highest authorities reject the Moorish hypothesis, and see in the Morris the survival of some primitive religious ceremonial." The self-assurance of this statement does much to conceal the trail of cloudy logic, dubious premises and discarded alternatives that went into its making, but two of the components should be brought out into the light.

1) The belief that morris is, or at least has its roots in, a pan-European custom. [This surprising opinion is probably intended to tighten the link between morris and the ceremonies of a rather misty peasant past. Sharp's source was quite obviously Douce, who is not the easiest of authors to understand, but a re-reading of the entry for 1807 might help.]

2) The acceptance that Cotswold morris is derived from the sword dances of north-east England and that the sacrificial element that can reasonably be deduced from some of the sword dances is also present [though invisible] in Cotswold dance.

Such was the power and range of Cecil Sharp's influence that this belief in morris as a pre-Christian religious rite met little challenge and became the backcloth against which later ideas about the morris were presented.

Cecil Sharp goes on to summarise his views on the nature and purpose of the primitive religious ceremonial that gave birth to morris dancing: views that are a clear echo from Sir James Frazer and Sir Edward Tylor.

> Shortly, however, we may explain that it was one of the seasonal pagan observances prevalent amongst primitive communities, and associated in some occult way with the fertilization of all living things, animal and vegetable. The central act of the ceremony was the slaughter of a sacred animal to provide a solemn sacramental feast. The primitive mind did not draw any clear line between its dimly-conceived clan-deity, the human members of the clan, and the sacred animals of the clan-herd. All were of one kindred, and the object of the sacrifice of the holy animal and the subsequent feast was to cement the bond between the god and the members of the clan.

As emotional fuel to drive forward Sharp's folk dance revival this may have been great stuff, but as history, it is bunk!

1934 – Rodney Gallop

For more than two hundred and sixty years people had been speculating upon the relationship between English morris and the Moorish dances of Spain and Portugal: so we might show slight surprise when we discover that the 1930s had arrived before anybody thought of going to look at the ceremonial dances that were still being performed there, and to see how they compared with the morris that we know in England. Rodney Gallop and Violet Alford were among the first in this field and Gallop published some of his findings in a paper called 'The Origins of the Morris Dance' (*JEFDSS* 1934). In his natural enthusiasm for his chosen subject he lays rather more stress on apparent similarities than he does upon the many obvious differences; however, before being too critical, it would be polite to remember that he was writing for the general climate of opinion in the 1930s when a more romantic approach to these matters was in favour.

Cecil Sharp had seen in the morris "the survival of some primitive religious ceremonial". Rodney Gallop was in full agreement and clearly believed that the same description was also applicable to the Iberian material. Since both these dance traditions had this deep and powerful underlying theme in common, superficial differences in the observed performances could not shake their fundamental sameness. A few moments' thought will reveal that this chain of argument has several weak links. At Pedrogão Pequeno in Portugal we are told:

> Seven men entered the church on St. John's Day, exotically dressed in silk and wearing conical hats decorated with flowers. Two of them played guitars, two tambourines and two carried wands surmounted by carnations. The seventh was called the King of Mourisca and bore a sword, a shield, a royal mantle and a crown. Bowing low before the statue of the Saint, all seven executed a slow and decorous dance at the conclusion of which they fell to their knees, while the King, pirouetting on one foot, shouted, 'Long live St. John the Baptist'.

I find both the detail and the spirit of this performance quite unlike any English morris I have ever seen or heard of, and only the use of the word 'Mourisca' brings it within the scope of this present study. Elsewhere in his paper the confidence of the 1930s rings through in statements like, "The 'Turks' are shown by their costume to be pure Morris dancers with little switches and tall plumed head-dresses, and their frequent battles with the Christians are danced to the accompaniment of music." This conviction that there was a close link between morris and certain Iberian folk performances reached a peak in 1958 when Lucile Armstrong wrote, "First hand knowledge of Pyrenean and Spanish traditional dances seems to me essential before publishing a study of English traditional 'Morris' dances." Mr Gallop draws attention to the "numerous ceremonial combats between Christians and Moors or Turks, all more or less choreographic in form, which are still today a feature of religious festivals from Portugal in the West to the eastern shores of the Adriatic" and goes on to note the great diversity of the performances that bear the name 'morisco'. He also sees other dances throughout Europe that seem to fall into the same classification although they bear a different name. In his attempts to pin down morisco, he laments the absence of any unifying features: even bells and blackface "are not sufficiently universal to warrant the assumption that either of them is essential to the dance." His valuable study of contemporary Iberian folk dance has been clouded, somewhat, by his attempt to weld centuries of Spanish and Portuguese folk performance, together with the English morris tradition, into one coherent whole. It is not surprising that we hear him protesting as he sinks slowly into a sea of loose ends.

There is however one line of thought offered in Gallop's paper that I find to be of particular interest. He says that in parts of Portugal a new-born child, before baptism, is called a 'mouro': sprites or fairies are known as 'mouras'; megalithic chamber tombs are 'antas de mouros' (caves of the

Moors) and archaeological remains, sherds, et cetera, are 'coisas de mouros' (things of the Moors). He suggests from this evidence that the word 'moorish' is used as a synonym for 'pagan', and since "It is unquestioned that the sacred dance was a part of pagan ritual before it was assimilated by the Christian church" it is reasonable to assume that the label 'moorish' was attached to these dances because of their pre-Christian origin. A 'morris' dance therefore means a 'pagan' dance and "We can assume that the Morris dance is not of Moorish origin". It is a sad conclusion from a man whose heart is so obviously in the other camp.

1935 – Violet Alford

Miss Alford presented a paper called 'Morris and Morisca' to the English Folk Dance and Song Society in 1935. This paper gives us some insight into the way many of the people interested in folklore were thinking during the inter-war years. A dance for men only, performed on a special day and in special costume, was deemed to be ceremonial, and a ceremonial dance was a short step away from a ritual dance. This thread of ritual function was then seen as running through certain folk customs across a wide spread of Europe, giving a kind of unity to dances from widely separated areas. (The laws of language require a ceremonial dance to relate to a ceremony and a ritual dance to a rite, but little attention was given to this aspect.)

Miss Alford's examination of the Iberian material led her to conclude that the term 'morisca' was a very loose one, covering a wide range of events. Nevertheless, one theme was frequently encountered – the dance/battle between Moors and Christians. This theme was widespread in southern Europe while, in parallel, the blacking of the face in imitation of the Moors had become a matter of fashion. The Moor/Christian battle never came to England, but the fact that a blackface tradition was already here (seen as a form of ritual disguise) has proved a fertile ground for confusion. She saw the moriscas as springing up on the heels of the retreating Moors and repeating, in dance form, the successful battles of Christian against Moor: the swords of these battles gradually transforming into sticks. The early moriscas were believed by Miss Alford to be court displays or entertainments, which in due course inspired the lower social classes to copy their betters and form a folk morisca. The court dance faded away, leaving the folk version which had, by then, grafted itself onto a set of earlier, seasonal and pre-Christian folk rituals. This view is admirably summed up in her last sentence: "English Morris and Continental Moriscas overlaid a seasonal, dancing rite in existence long before either Moors or Christians had entered Europe". It is, of course, nearly two thousand years since Christians entered Europe. On a more cautious note, it is fourteen hundred years since Spain was converted from Arian Christianity to Roman Catholicism and thirteen hundred since the Moors entered Spain. Thus we were expected (in 1935) to believe that at the root of morris there lay a dance that was ritual, seasonal and of very great age. Indeed, one gets a strong feeling that even to enquire into these three basic precepts would have been not quite the done thing.

1936 – Dr Joseph Needham

Soon after the serious study of morris dancing had begun in the early years of the twentieth century it became quite clear that English ceremonial dances came in different sorts, and that the 'sort' depended upon the part of the country the dance came from. Labels like 'Northwest' and 'Cotswold' are a natural consequence of this obviously geographical arrangement. Dr Needham brought an element of precision to the subject by gathering together all references he could find to ceremonial dances that had been performed since 1800: he classified these dances into types and plotted the locations on a map. The results of his study were published as 'The Geographical Distribution of English Ceremonial Dance Traditions' (*JEFDSS* 1936).

Dr Needham drew attention to interesting similarities between his map showing the distribution of dance types, and the areas of political division that existed before the Norman conquest. Sword dances occur in the eastern counties where Scandinavian influence had been strong: Rapper dances in Northumbria to the north of the Tees, and Longsword in the Yorkshire lands of the Danelaw. Molly dances also occur within the Danish lands and although the surviving fragments of this tradition are based on country dances, there are hints that in older times Molly may also have contained a sword dance element. Those styles of dance to which the word 'morris' is most firmly attached – Cotswold, Northwest and Border – all come from the lands of Anglian Mercia. Wessex, south of the Thames, is notable for a total absence of any ceremonial dance, along with Essex, Suffolk and Norfolk. (Perhaps a case could be made that Danes and Angles danced, but Saxons and Jutes did not.) Maytime processional dances (the Helston Furry Dance is the best-known example) seem to have their home in the old Celtic lands of Cornwall and Wales. It is not entirely clear what historical conclusion ought to be drawn from Dr Needham's observations, for the political boundaries he uses were established in the ninth century and were obliterated in 1066. If we discount coincidence, then two possibilities might be put forward rather cautiously.

1) Ninth-century immigrants from various parts of Denmark and north Germany practised a variety of different styles of dance and the distinctive features of these dances persisted for a thousand years. The evidence is not sufficient to decide whether they brought these traditions with them from their homelands, or whether they started to dance only after they reached England.

and

2) Angle remained culturally distinct from Dane until such time as they chose to adopt (or invent) a tradition of dance.

Dr Needham then goes on to consider two current theories about the origin of morris in the light of his geographical studies. The first, which was propounded by Cecil Sharp and expanded by Violet Alford, saw morris (i.e. Cotswold morris) as a development from sword dancing of the Rapper or Longsword type. They saw metal swords becoming wooden swords becoming sticks becoming handkerchiefs. The second theory, put forward by Phillips Barker, saw morris developing out of processional dances – the usual Cotswold starting figure, the Foot Up, was perhaps a remnant of the procession. This idea was built up until a Cotswold set dance could be seen as the priestly head of a procession from which the tail had disappeared. Needham came down firmly on the side of processional origins and he was convinced that there was a difference in substance between morris and the sword dances. However, with the benefit of a good dose of hindsight, we can see both theories as products of a widespread academic fashion of the 1930s – a desire to arrange things in a 'developmental sequence'. An author would lay out his items of evidence in what he felt was an order of logical change and then go on to claim that this was the time order in which things happened. The pitfalls in such a method are fairly obvious, particularly in the unpredictable world of folk customs.

1937 – Curt Sachs

Curt Sachs' large volume, *World History of the Dance* (published 1937) devotes eight pages to a discussion of moresque and morris, presenting a medley of fact and imagination illustrated with a welter of examples that often hinder as much as help the theme being developed. Sachs, like Frazer, seems to enjoy a world-wide ethnographic paper-chase. As he pursues hobby-horses from the English morris to the Balearic Islands, to Java, to the north of ancient China and so on, the reader is left breathless and wondering just what he is supposed to conclude from such a tour. Nevertheless Curt Sachs has things to say that are worthy of our careful attention. Under the heading, 'Europe Since Antiquity', he writes:

The moresque is the most frequently mentioned of all the dances of the fifteenth century. Whether balls, masquerades, or ballets are described, such names as basse danse, saltarello, and piva are seldom mentioned, it is almost always stated that the participants danced a morisca. Yet this dance is one of the most difficult to classify and characterize in all dance history. Morisco is the Spanish name for a Moor who after the country was reconquered remained there and became a Christian. *The moresque, therefore, must be understood primarily as the shape which the romantic memories of the Moorish period in southern Europe took in the dance.* It appears first in two forms: as a solo dance of approximately the type which might have been performed by dancers at the Moorish courts, and as a couple or group dance in which the motif was a sword combat between the Christians and the Mohammedans. [My italics]

He notes that the name *morisca* is also used for dances that do not have this motif of religious violence. (Could it be that these were the dances that were once danced by the Moors themselves: as opposed to the combat dances where the unvarying defeat of the Moors makes it clear that the performers were Christian?) "By a strange irony of fate the moresque, the most exotic element in the medieval dance, has in Europe given, if not its theme, at least its name to the national dance of a very un-Moorish and un-Spanish people." He identifies the English morris dance and goes on:

Its characteristic form since the fifteenth century has been a group usually of six men with a fool, a boy dressed as a woman – Mayde Maryan – and another man carrying around his hips the cardboard figure of a horse. All of them wear fantastic costumes hung with many bells. Blacking of the face is also common. The musician has a flute and a small drum or a bagpipe, today often a violin or an accordion.

This belief in five hundred years of little change, and the bias of the picture towards the Cotswold form of morris, both suggest the influence of Cecil Sharp. Sachs also follows Sharp into the trap of linking sixteenth-century French moresque with present English morris on the strength of Arbeau's tune.

The hobby-horse theme leads Mr Sachs to consider the Calusari (a custom from Romania in which groups of men visit the homes around their village with a performance so strange and difficult to define that the word 'ritual' flows naturally from the pen. They have sometimes been called Hobby Horse Dancers because one of the possible interpretations of their name equates 'calus' to 'little horse'). He then moves on to generalise about fertility rites that "were already developed in the Early Tribal cultures of the Miolithic period". (This takes us back eight thousand years! I wonder how he gets his evidence.) Two motifs of these old fertility rites he sees as the blacking of the face and the combat between two sides. "Thus," he concludes, "the concept of the moresque is for the most part nothing but a late revaluation of ancient fertility ceremonies."

This discussion, like so many others in the literature, turns, not on the dance itself, but upon attendant features: in this particular instance, on hobby-horses, blackface and combat. Before being swept along by a story eloquently told, it is well to pause and consider how valid are the links between the dance and these attendant features. Morris, for Mr Sachs, seems to be Cotswold morris and it just so happens that the Cotswold morris noted from traditional performers has no hobby-horses, no blackface and no element of combat! This is not to say that Sachs is totally wrong, for these elements do occur, particularly in the earlier records, and they will be considered in some detail later in this book: but whether or not they form an adequate support for his conclusion is left to the reader.

1955 and 1957 – Barbara Lowe

For years, morris had been seen by a lot of people as a part of folklore, and the faint whiff of the fairies that hangs around the word 'folklore' had brushed off onto the morris. It is therefore refreshing to find in the articles of Barbara Lowe that the mists have been swept aside and items of evidence are now set up in full view so readers are given some chance to judge for themselves and agree, or disagree, with her interpretations. Mrs Lowe has rendered a great service to all those interested in early morris by gathering together most of the references to morris in England during its first two hundred years – from the earliest mention in 1458, up to the time of the Civil War. (See 'Early Records of the Morris in England', *JEFDSS* 1957.) Mrs Lowe's work is one of the firmer foundations upon which this book is based.

In an earlier paper, 'Robin Hood in the Light of History', read in 1954 (published *JEFDSS* 1955), Mrs Lowe described some of the background against which the morris developed. Read together, these two papers give a good idea of the various influences that were circulating in the early part of the sixteenth century, when morris first began to appear at the May Games and in other parish festivities. There were court moriscas; lords of misrule; official concern for military weapons training; the plays of Robin Hood, and not forgetting those familiar characters, Fool, Maid Marian and Hobby-Horse.

40

1979 – Matthew Alexander

The first issue of a magazine called *Southern Rag* had an article under the heading 'Morris – The Origins' written by Matthew Alexander. Mr Alexander introduces the ancient-pagan-fertility-ritual theory of morris origins and points to the mismatch that exists between the theory and the evidence. This leads him to suggest,"The modern Morris might not be continuing an ancient pagan rite, but may be the stylised and faded remnants of a gorgeous royal spectacle". Mr Alexander is a dancer and his writing is perhaps less seriously presented than that of other authors in this Guide, but nevertheless, the point he raises is worthy of some consideration. It is hoped that the balance of the possibilities will become clearer as this book progresses. In the next issue of *Southern Rag* Alexander examines the 'Morris in Surrey', looking at the scanty fragments of morris history in his own county: parish fundraising activities in Tudor times; Vinckenboom's painting of morris dancers at Richmond around 1620; and on to what seems to have become, by the mid-1800s, a solo dance commonly performed by chimney sweeps.

1999 – John Forrest

A study of morris history has always been a bit like trying to find needles in the haystack of world literature and the last fifteen years have seen Keith Chandler, Michael Heaney and John Forrest become very effective in this hunt. This body of work has yielded a number of publications, but the first to offer itself to a wider public is *The History of Morris Dancing 1458 – 1750* by John Forrest.

John Forrest writes in an academic style, skilfully handling large quantities of data, but the sheer mass of his material makes it a fairly hard-work read. He regularly gives warnings to his readers about the sparsity of evidence in a particular area, or to its lack of clarity, but the more general reader may find it difficult to separate the evidence from the author's personal interpretations, and when evidence plus interpretation is used as foundation for the next step, some chains of development look much stronger in this book than my view of the material would support. A detailed analysis would not be appropriate here, but a very rough sketch of a single item might serve by way of example. Tournament changed over the years from hard battle practice to a colourful show where costume, scenery and a fanciful plot entertained an audience, while the fighting had become comparatively safe. Elsewhere, there is the show that I think of as ring morris and which John Forrest calls morisk, where four or five dancers cavort around a lady holding a ring. The tournament can be seen as young men proclaiming a set-piece love of women as they charge into combat for a prize. The dancers are indulging in a personal display in the hope, presumably, of winning the ring. John sees a theme flowing from tournament to morris. Well – perhaps. Or is an enthusiasm for the evolutionary model getting the upper hand? Then readers who are not making notes as they go along might see Maid Marian taking over from the lady with the ring and instead of giving a prize, she becomes the prize: this leads Forrest to go some way in agreement with the puritan Phillip Stubbes (1583) because, as he says, "The sexual themes in the church-sponsored morris of the time were so blatant" (p.188). A strong statement indeed, bearing in mind that there is no clear evidence for Maid Marian ever taking part in a church-sponsored morris dance. This urge to find linkages may well lie at the root of his somewhat discourteous attitude toward some of the performances. The word 'parody' rises too easily to his pen.

Notwithstanding my comments, this is a book with many valuable features, and I would particularly like to offer thanks to John Forrest for his contribution to the 'Pre-Christian origins of morris' debate. I can do no better than quote from page 190:

The actual link in the Elizabethan mind between paganism and popery, going back to Polydor Vergil, was the city of Rome. Elizabethan Puritans, when they spoke of paganism, did not mean any pre-Christian culture (and certainly not pre-Christian Britain), but were specifically referring to Ancient Rome, pagan capital of the classical world. According to a well-known Reformation argument, the Catholic church, because its capital was Rome, had become heir to the paganism of that city, and thus, a great many traditions of the Roman church (including traditional sports and recreations) were seen as descendants of pagan customs.

CHAPTER 2: REVIEW OF EARLIER WORK
Summary

CHAPTER 3

THE SPANISH CONNECTION

The word *morris* comes from the Spanish word *morisco* – of that there is no reasonable doubt. Look up *morisco* in a Spanish/English dictionary and you will find that it means 'Moorish'. Morris, therefore, is a Moorish dance come by way of Spain – or is it?

Francis Peck, in 1740, clearly believed that it was; but whether or not he had any evidence to support his belief, we do not know. He may well have considered it self-evident that a dance called 'Moorish' must have come from the Moors. If this was the case, then his story about John of Gaunt may have been no more than a plausible background added to a foregone conclusion. Today, stories of Moorish origins are still occasionally heard among morris dancers and it may be that it is Peck's account, kept circulating by later writers, that is the foundation on which all these stories stand. However, be that as it may, at this point I want to leave the Spanish question standing unanswered for a while – until we have had a chance to mull over some more of the facts and possibilities.

Let us assume (for the moment) that there *was* a link between Moorish Spain and the English morris. Our study then requires us to know a little bit about the Moors and why they were in Spain, and to give some consideration as to how a Spanish dance could have been so successfully transplanted into English soil. English people are not renowned for their understanding of continental history: most will have heard of Aragon (Catherine of), Agincourt (Laurence Olivier) and Granada (Ford Motor Company); but few could fit these names into an unrolling flow of history. For this reason I am putting together some crib notes under four headings: headings that *may* have some relevance to the history of morris.

The Moors in Spain

A few years after the death of Mahommet in 632 AD the Arabs started to expand out of Arabia: to the east, to the north and, more important for this story, westward along the coast of North Africa. The Berbers in Morocco halted the advance for a while but were then converted to Islam, whereupon the forces of the Prophet swept on and up into Spain. By 714 AD almost the whole of the Spanish peninsula had been brought under Muslim control. The people who fell under this Muslim control were Visigoths who had been in Spain ever since the Roman Empire failed in the fifth century and who had followed the Roman Catholic faith for well over a hundred years at the time of their defeat.

The driving force behind this Muslim move into Spain was the wish to get their hands on the tax potential of an economically successful country (a common enough reason for conquest in any age). Our history books may give the impression of a great struggle between rival religions, but this is a version of the story that takes colour from the fundraising publicity of kings and princes planning for their next conquest. The ordinary people in their day to day lives would have seen a much less dramatic picture. There were some differences, of course: the arrival of the Muslims meant relief from the rigidity of law and taxation that the Visigoths had inherited from the Romans; the Jews were no longer persecuted; and slaves, who formed a large and vital part of the Christian economy, could win their freedom by getting converted to Islam. But generally, a large part of the population remained Christian and continued their everyday business unmolested. Taking the broadest of broad views, and with the religious tolerance of recent years, we might reasonably assess the victory of Moor over Christian as a good thing.

The government of the Arabian empire rested in the hands of an aristocratic family called the Umayyads until 749 AD when authority passed on to another family of more Persian sympathies. But Spain, being across the water, remained true to the Umayyads and declared herself independent of the empire in 756. Changes in political control were many and varied throughout the main lands of the Arabian empire, but the Umayyads in Spain were a stable feature that went on in comparatively unruffled isolation for nearly three hundred years, during which time the Muslim component of the population rose to around twenty per cent. (The total population of Spain at this time was something like four million.) By 1000 AD the old tensions between Berber and Arab were edging Spain towards civil war and the Christian kings of the north were not slow to take advantage of this situation. The capture of Toledo in 1085 can be seen as the first major step in the Reconquest. This external pressure caused the Muslims to re-unite, with the result that the Christian advance was very, very slow, taking a hundred and eighty years to squeeze the main part of the Moorish forces out of Spain.

By 1269, Islam in Spain had been reduced to a small strip on the southern coast calling itself the 'Emirate of Granada'. A map of the main political boundaries at this date would show that Portugal occupied something like its modern area; Castile held the central bulk of the country; Aragon lay along the east coast; while Navarre was tucked away at the western end of the Pyrenees. This map of 1269 persisted with very little change until Ferdinand, heir to Aragon, married Isabella, heiress to Castile, in 1469: a marriage that provided Henry VIII with his first wife and created the Spain we all know, famous for the Armada and package holidays. The fall of Granada in 1492 marks the end of our story with the final extinction of Moorish control in Spain, seven hundred and eighty-one years after the first arrival.

This tale requires a postscript: for although we have looked at the end of Moorish political and military power in Spain, there was no immediate exodus. When the Reconquest reached its completion there were still more than a million Muslims in the country, and a similar number of Jews. As the need for military action declined, so religious zeal found other outlets and the doctrine of Catholic Uniformity grew in strength: Jews went back to being persecuted, and Muslims were threatened with deportation. Under such pressures, many took the easy way out and accepted baptism into the Christian Church (these baptised Muslims were called Moriscos and the Jews, Marranos). It is hardly surprising that many of these converts lacked enthusiasm for their new religion, and the Spanish Inquisition was founded in 1480 with a first duty to attend to backsliding among these Marranos and Moriscos. At first, only those who insisted upon openly practising the religion of their forefathers earned deportation: Jews were expelled from the country in 1492 and some Muslims in 1502. But as time went on, standards were tightened up until it became necessary to demonstrate Christian ancestors for four generations back, before a man could rely on keeping out of the hands of the Inquisition. Various edicts were issued during the sixteenth century for the deportation of Muslims and Moriscos, culminating with the ejection of a quarter of a million of them in the years 1609–1614.

Our story requires us to note that here were substantial numbers of people of Moorish origin, many known as Moriscos, being pushed out of Spain to find homes in (presumably) non Catholic countries. Perhaps some earned a living by dancing.

John of Gaunt (1340–1399)

> The morris or moorish dance was first brought into England, as I take it, in Edward III time, when John of Gaunt returned from Spain.
> (Peck, 1740)

In 1367, John of Gaunt, Duke of Lancaster, son of Edward III, led a strong military force to the assistance of Peter the Cruel, King of Castile, who was fighting his brother for the crown. This attempt by John to win a stake in Castile by force of arms was a failure, so he adopted another strategy and married King Peter's elder daughter. (It has been said that John brought his wife back to live in Tutbury Castle, and perhaps these Moorish dances were introduced for her entertainment.) Peter was murdered in 1369 and John of Gaunt spent sixteen years trying to press his claim (by marriage) to the crown of Castile. But again he met with no success and eventually settled for no more than a marriage between his daughter and the Castilian heir.

With these interests in Castile and his involvement in English politics John of Gaunt must have 'returned from Spain' on a number of occasions. History notes such journeys in 1367, 1374, 1389 and 1395. King Edward died in 1377, so if we take Peck to be literally true, then the last two dates are invalid and we have a choice between 1367 and 1374. The gap of eighty-four years between 1374 and the earliest surviving mention of morris in England is perhaps a shade long for us to be entirely comfortable with this theory for the introduction of morris.

The English in France

Writers have pointed out that English lords and soldiers ruled in south-west France at the same time as the Moors were in Spain, and it has been suggested that this may have been the route by which morris travelled to England.

It is almost universal knowledge that the Normans conquered England in 1066: it is rather less well known that England conquered Normandy some forty years later. Brittany had been settled from Britain in the sixth century and still retained some fellow feeling for the parent country, and in any case Brittany was politically dependent on Normandy. Add to this situation the wedding of Henry I's daughter to the Count of Anjou which produced a son (Henry II) heir to both Anjou and England; Henry II then went on to improve his fortunes even further by marrying Eleanor of Aquitaine. If we go on to note that by this time Anjou and Aquitaine had between them absorbed all the other provinces of western France, then we can see how Henry II came to the throne of England in 1154 and was lord over more land in France than was held by the French king himself: a dominion won by skilful marriage rather than by the sword. Fortune favoured the English indeed – even the Pope was an Englishman.

In fairness to the politics of the time it should perhaps be said that Henry II, great-grandson of William the Conqueror, would not have thought of himself as just an English King. Even less would he have considered himself to be an Englishman. He was an Angevin King who was fortunate enough to include England within his Dominions.

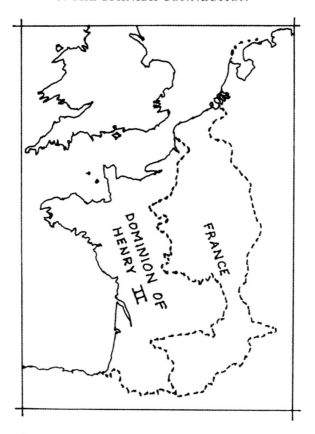

Sixty years later, these English lands in France had been reduced to a coastal strip along the southern half of the western seaboard; then for another two hundred years these south-western possessions waxed and waned in a fairly minor way until, in 1415, Agincourt won most of northern France for England. But this success was short-lived. Joan of Arc turned the tide against England and in 1453 the last of the English forces were expelled from France (except for Calais) and the Hundred Years' War was over.

Our present view of morris as a folk custom leads us to seek its history among the villages at a time when the history books have little more to offer us than tales of the aristocracy and high-level politics like those outlined above. We can do no more than speculate about the sort of social contact that might have led to a transfer of dance information. The first point of possible contact was the soldier. English soldiers were in France for three hundred years – say fifteen generations of service men. Some will have made friends with the locals, and the occasional soldier must surely have brought home a French, Spanish or Basque wife. (Direct contact with the Moors seems unlikely, because when the English arrived in France around

49

1154 the Moors were already in retreat and a hundred and fifty miles of Christian Spanish kingdom separated Englishman from Moor.) At the very least, the substantial number of returned soldiers would have formed a knowledgeable audience for any dances of the Franco-Spanish border that may have been performed in England. Secondly, the movement of Dukes and Kings through these lands would have brought traders, officials, envoys, messengers and minor nobility following along in their wake: men who might be expected to have a better than average intelligence and education. It is possible that a man of this sort took an interest in local customs sufficient to note down, or even learn the dances. A third possibility, and the only one for which there is any shred of evidence, turns on the custom of top people giving lavish entertainments for high-ranking visitors. It was a fashionable attraction in such entertainments to have a display of dancing by 'savages', and it seems quite likely that on some occasions at least, the savages were what we would call folk dancers, brought in from a nearby town or village, paid a fee that was large by peasant standards and kitted out with fancy dress to suit the theme of the evening.

Before leaving these speculations on the method of transfer, it is as well to remind ourselves that large numbers of people were not necessary: a single person (and one thinks of someone like Cecil Sharp, or Roy Dommett) moving from Spain to England at the right time could have transplanted an entire tradition of dance – and one journey by one man or woman of common rank is unlikely to have left a trace in history. Little more can be said about the English military presence in France in this hypothetical role as a bridge connecting the customs of Moorish Spain to the ceremonial dances of England. But before we leave the Anglo-French battlefields, there is one more point which may prove to be very important indeed.

The first half of the fourteenth century saw several important changes in the techniques of war. For one thing, firearms were introduced, but they were slow to get going and had no great importance until the next century. A change with much more impact was the adoption of the longbow: this sent echoes throughout the whole of contemporary society. Edward I had come across the longbow while campaigning in Wales around 1280 and, foreseeing its value, he had it adopted for the English army. Guided first by Edward, and then by the tactical skill of his grandson Edward III, the archers of the English army grew in reputation until the battle of Crécy in 1346 demonstrated, with no remaining possibility for doubt, that an army with a strong force of longbowmen could defeat any army that still pinned its hope on men-at-arms. These men-at-arms (the 'knights in shining armour' of romantic literature) had been dominant figures on the mediaeval battlefield, and a moment's thought will suggest that equipping such men and their horses must have been a matter of very great expense. It follows that the fighting men would have been drawn from the sons and servants of the upper classes. On the other hand, the essential equipment of a longbowman could be made in a couple of hours, or bought for a shilling. So the ranks of the archers were made up from artisans, from the sons of yeoman farmers, and from village labourers: people strong in the arm and independent of noble patronage.

From this we can see the shattering effect that Crécy had upon society: for the very first time, the commoners were more to be feared than the lords. King and Council became aware of their dependence upon villagers, and interest began to be shown in the happiness, goodwill and patriotic spirit within village life. Village games were organised with feasting, drinking and jollifications interspersed with archery competitions and the exercise of other military skills. Into these festivities came Robin Hood, followed not long after by the morris dancers.

By a coincidence of history, only three years after Crécy, a very different event came along which also had the effect of lifting the importance of villagers. The Black Death cut down one third of the population and pushed up the price of labour.

The Basques

I have already drawn attention to the close similarity that exists today between the Cotswold morris and certain of the Basque dances. If we go on to note that, of the three episodes of history considered in this chapter so far, all have taken place quite close to the Basque homelands – then there are sufficient hints lying around to warrant a few thoughts about the Basques.

The Basques are different. Everybody seems to think so – especially the Basques. If we try to account for this feeling of difference, two principal factors emerge. First comes their language. All European languages can be traced back to a misty common root-stock called by linguists 'Indo-European' – all, that is, except for Basque, which stands by itself: of unknown origin. Secondly, the Basque people have an enduring permanence – they have always been there. If we imagine the map of Europe through the eye of a high-speed ciné camera and see two thousand years of history pass in a few minutes, we would see peoples expand, contract, merge, split, migrate or disappear under a multitude of political, military and economic influences. All is change and all is movement – except for the area around the western end of the Pyrenees which is now, as it was at the time of Christ, the home of the Basques.

Medical research has now added a strand of scientific respectability to this belief in the uniqueness of the Basques, for it has noted that the rhesus-negative factor, used in classifying blood, which occurs in 15 per cent of an average European group, occurs in 40 per cent of the Basques.

The Basques have not been well treated by those who draw political boundaries, and the Basque country has always been crossed by other people's frontiers. Nevertheless they have remained a coherent people who have been little changed by Romans or by Visigoths or by Muslims or by any of the other later disturbances. It has been suggested that the Basques are the aboriginal Europeans – here before the rest of us came – and it would be natural to expect such a people to be the repository of some very old traditions.

What links can we now envisage between the Basque people and England? A company of Basques and Gascons[1] are recorded as fighting for Edward I in his wars against the Welsh around 1280. The Atlantic sea routes have usually permitted easy trade between the two countries and England has certainly imported Basque fruit and iron ore over long periods of time. Gascony was under English rule from 1360 to 1451 (and for part of that time it was ruled by John of Gaunt's brother). It is therefore clear enough that contact of some sort took place, but whether a dance changed hands, and at what date, and in which direction, we cannot say.

When God needed some bones with which to make the first man,
He took them from a Basque cemetery.
(Basque Legend)

[1] The Gascons are an offshoot of the Basque people who moved north of the Pyrenees in the sixth century.

CHAPTER 4

WHAT'S IN THE NAME?
An inquiry into pre-Christian origins

Under the heading of 'The Spanish Connection' we have already had a look at the historical scenery that would apply if morris came from Moorish Spain. This seems a convenient place at which to change hats and say, 'What if it didn't?' One immediate effect is to wipe out the easy line of thought that runs: morris is called morris because it comes from the Moors. If it didn't, we need another reason why morris is called morris. Strutt, in 1801, called into question the Moorish origin of the dances and a number of other writers have shared his doubts, but the derivation of the *word* has never been seriously challenged. The word link, morris – morisco – moorish, seems to hold good. Why, then, did an English dance come to be called moorish if it didn't come from the Moors? Perhaps we need to look for a rather more subtle meaning for the word moorish.

Folklorists are usually keen to emphasise the antiquity of the customs that catch their interest, and this has led several to take a hint from Peck and suggest that the name *morris* (or *morisco*) was brought into England and added to a pre-existing dance custom. By this means the dance custom can be seen as running back into the golden haze of the past, neatly sidestepping around the terminal dates imposed by Moorish history. It is at this point that blacking the face becomes important again. The obvious interpretation of blackface is that the dances were Moorish and the performers were trying to look like Moors, but our present line of enquiry requires a different solution. A widely accepted belief runs something like this.

An ancient dance was a component in some pre-Christian ritual. Now for the magic to work in such a ritual it was necessary for the performers to be disguised (for nobody would expect the Elements to change their ways for Young Fred – but changes might happen in response to the Ritual Dancers). One of the easiest ways to disguise oneself was to wear unusual clothes, perhaps a jacket turned inside out, and then black the face with charcoal. Thus, when the idea came into this country that a man with a black face was called a Moor, these ritual dancers with blackened faces came to be called moorish dancers. As Sir Edmund Chambers put it in *The Mediaeval Stage* (1903), "I would suggest that the faces were not blackened because the dancers represented Moors, but rather the dancers were thought to represent Moors because their faces were blackened."

Concealing the face has often been linked with supernatural powers. The word sequence, visor – visard – wizard, opens up one line of speculation, while another line turns on the word 'grim'. Among the roots of this word lies the idea of covering the lower part of the face with forearm and cloak. The great god Woden walked the world in this manner and so came to be called Grim, a name which persists on our landscape, where Iron Age ditches are commonly given the name 'Grimsdyke'.

We have seen in Rodney Gallop's 1934 paper that he suggested the word *moorish* might have been used in the sense of 'pagan'; if this was so, then a pre-Christian dance was a moorish dance by definition and all that is left for us to imagine is the transfer of the word, together with its special meaning, from Portugal to England.

The blackface disguise theory and Rodney Gallop's idea both require morris to be pre-Christian – and we recall how popular this belief has been through a large part of the twentieth century. So, when did England adopt Christianity? Here is a question without a simple answer, and a topic that has filled many books from the Venerable Bede onward. All that can be attempted here is a quick sketch.

The Beginnings of Christianity in England[1]

The Roman Catholic Church was dominant in this country from the Synod of Whitby in 663 until Henry VIII married Anne Boleyn in 1533. As a consequence, all accounts of early religion have had to pass through a Catholic filter eight and a half centuries long – a filter that was keen to eliminate anything that might be seen to compete with Roman primacy. One result of this fact is a scarcity of information about the Celtic Christianity that was well established in England for centuries before the arrival of Roman doctrine. A second result is the common belief that Pope Gregory sent Augustine to Britain in 596 to introduce Christianity to a pagan country.[2] There is an element of truth here, but a more careful look will suggest that his job was to convert the recently successful pagan invaders to Rome before they could be snapped up by the native Celtic Christian Church. The thin scatter of hints and clues that have survived to mark the early days of Christianity in England can be woven into a chronicle that runs something like this.

[1.] There was, of course, no England before the Angles. I use the word here to indicate the present-day geographical area.

[2.] Or, as a cynic might put it, to convert the people from Christianity to Roman Catholicism.

A strangely persistent legend tells a tale of Joseph of Arimathea: that he came to England in the year **63** AD, settled in Glastonbury, and built a church of wattle. This story is reinforced by a second legend that tells of the arrival of the Saxons in Glastonbury in 658. There they found a wattle building of forgotten origin that bore signs of much careful preservation. It was known as The Old Church (see Geoffrey Ashe, *King Arthur's Avalon*, 1957).

Bede records that in the time when Eleutherius was Pope (**167–182**), Lucius, a British king, sent him a letter, asking to be made a Christian. This pious request was quickly granted, and the Britons held the Faith which they received in all its purity and fullness until the time of the Emperor Diocletian (284). Unfortunately, Lucius is not known to history, and a king of any sort in Roman Britain seems a bit unlikely.

Uncertainty surrounds the date of death for our first Christian martyr, St Alban: **208** AD, or shortly after **250**, are the present best guesses. The event clearly shows the presence in England of an illegal Christian minority.

That great theologian and teacher of the ancient church, Origen (**185–254**), wrote: "When did the land of Britain ever unite in the belief of one God, before Christ came?" This seems to imply that, in Alexandria, Britain was looked upon as a Christian country.

In the year **313** the Roman Emperor Constantine issued an Edict of Toleration which permitted Christianity to be practised (he was himself baptised a Christian on his deathbed in **337**). Then in **380** Christianity was made the official Roman religion. From this time onwards we may expect Roman soldiers and officials to be Christian, in name at least.

The great Council of Arles held in **314** was attended by three bishops from Britain (one from London, one from York and one who probably came from either Colchester or Lincoln). Another Council at Rimini in **359** also had British bishops in attendance.

The period from **337** to **400** saw Christianity increasing in popularity among the upper classes – in the army, in the towns and in the villas. In these places Christianity and paganism existed side by side, but the country areas stayed overwhelmingly pagan – indeed, the word pagan means countryman.

The first British thinker to make his mark in the Christian record was the heretic Pelagius (**350–420**), who disagreed with the doctrine of inherited sin and upset the orthodox Church by claiming that God had provided each man with sufficient wit and will to guide himself through a sinful world and that Divine judgement would be based on his performance, not on some predetermined gift of grace. This theme of self-reliance was also strongly relevant to the politics of the time – for the Romans were departing and leaving Britain to fight her own battles. (As a sidelight on attitudes of the day, Jerome, writer of the Vulgate version of the Bible, called Pelagius "a corpulent dog weighed down with Scottish porridge ".[1])

The period **409** to **449** was one of uneasy peace without the accustomed security of Roman protection: a period that was marked by a constant conflict within the upper levels of society between the orthodox and the Pelagian views on Christianity.

Tradition has it that Hengist and Horsa came to this country in **449** in response to an invitation from Vortigern, but the situation soon deteriorated into war, with Christian-led British forces trying to resist the advance of pagan Anglo-Saxons. King Arthur's famous victory at Mount Badon circa **518** brought this period to a close and fixed a frontier giving the Anglo-Saxons control over the eastern third of England and much of the south, while Celtic Britons still held the middle and west. Somewhere within this period the Christian Church in Britain seems to have developed an individuality which set it at some variance with the Church of Rome.

Then followed two generations of peace (**518** to **570**) during which time Christianity spread downward through society and out across the countryside until, around **550**, all Britons were nominally Christian. Round about this time the Celtic Church moved strongly towards a monastic style of organisation.

Meanwhile, Christianity had travelled from England to Ireland with Saint Patrick (circa 430) and come back (bearing a strong Celtic flavour) with Columba, who founded a monastery on Iona in **563** as a bridgehead for the conversion of the people of the Northern Lands. It has been suggested that this evangelism by Columba and his monks reached rather more Anglo-Saxons than Bede would have us believe. There is also some evidence to suggest that the ruling families of the North had been in contact with Christianity for a very long while: perhaps from as far back as 400.

War broke out again in the period from **570** to **603**. The Anglo-Saxons resumed their advance and pushed the British forces back into Cornwall and Wales so that the Angles, Saxons and Jutes, between them, occupied almost the whole of England. The orthodox view holds that the Anglo-Saxons of this time were still totally pagan, but it is probably true that a military occupation of this sort drives away the soldiers, the leaders and the wealthy, but leaves the peasants to tend the same land for new landlords. It could thus be argued that here was a Christian peasantry living under pagan rule.

---

[1] Reported in Chadwick, *The Early Church.*

The celebrated arrival of Saint Augustine in this country in **597** led, in a fairly leisurely way, to the conversion of various groups of Saxons and Angles over the period from **627** to **686**. Rather more quietly and with signs of greater efficiency, the Celtic Church set up at Lindisfarne in **635** to work on the conversion of Northumbria. Then in **663**, the Synod of Whitby made the momentous decision that England would henceforward follow the Roman Church instead of the Celtic one and by **700** we can say that the whole country was essentially Christian. A point to note in passing is that the conversion of pagans had been fairly easy – the really difficult bits had been dealing with deviant Christians (like trying to persuade the Celtic Church to follow the Roman way of fixing a date for Easter, or getting agreement on the style of monastic haircut).

After many years of raiding and piracy the Danes adopted a policy of full-scale settlement around **865** and brought paganism back to England, spreading over the eastern third of the country between Thames and Tees. The military power of the Danes was expelled by **920**, leaving behind their more peaceable countrymen to form the Danelaw and drift quietly into Christianity. (The militant Danes and their Viking friends went away and moved into northern France, where they changed their name to 'Normans' and waited around for a century and a half before setting out on a much more successful attempt to occupy England.) In **927** the various kings of England and the North drew together under Athelstan with an undertaking to suppress idolatry, and for the first time England became one united kingdom.

A group of Irish Viking adventurers moved into the area round York as the Danes withdrew. They held it, on and off, until Eric Bloodaxe was expelled in **954**: an event which marked the end of the last community in this country to be officially pagan.

* * * * *

After that quick dash through the Dark Ages – that most difficult and uncertain period of English history – we can now sit back and consider the consequences of joining the idea of 'morris' onto the idea of 'pre-Christian'. It may be obvious, but it is probably a good idea to set it down in black and white – any dance which once formed part of a pre-Christian ritual must, necessarily, go back to a time before people adopted Christianity. We are now in a position to put some dates against this idea and list three alternative possibilities

Latest possible date for genuinely pre-Christian morris	Religion of dancers	Area
1. 550 AD (Thereafter converted to Christianity)	Pagan Celt	Middle and west of England
2. 700 AD (Thereafter converted to Christianity)	Pagan Angle	England (north of Thames)
3. 920 AD (Thereafter driven out of England)	Pagan Dane	Eastern England (Thames to Tees)

This table includes the usual assumption that morris is a matter for peasants and villagers and not for the upper classes; and, since there is no evidence for a concentration of morris around York, I have disregarded Eric Bloodaxe and his crew. Credit for dancing is given to the Angles, but not to the Saxons and Jutes, on the strength of Needham's work with dance distributions.

Two of the three possibilities in the table involve a boundary in roughly the same location – a north/south line dividing eastern England from the middle and west – and we can recall how Joseph Needham drew attention to a similar line when it separated Christian Angle from pagan Dane in the ninth century. Dr Needham went on to point out how neatly this line coincided with the eastern limit of Cotswold-style dances as shown by his plot of nineteenth-century performances. We are now in a position to weave these thoughts on dates, dance distributions and political boundaries into some very tentative suggestions.

1) Either:
   1A) Cotswold/Northwest/Border morris had its origins among the Celts before 550 AD.
Or:
   1B) Cotswold/Northwest/Border morris had its origins among the Angles before 700 AD and the tradition was later pushed back to the line by invading Danes.

2) Longsword/Molly dance was implanted by the Danes during their occupation from 865 to 920 AD.

This is an excellent time at which to cry Halt! For although the ideas may still run onward, the logic becomes woollier, the ground more insubstantial, and we need to remind ourselves that a full five hundred years still have to pass, after the latest date in this story, before we meet the first historical mention of morris in England. We also need to recall that this line of enquiry has been entirely dependent upon the assumption that morris started out as a pre-Christian religious ritual: an assumption we may not wish to endorse after looking the implications squarely in the face.

Anyone who fancies following the path a little further could with profit study Joseph Needham's 1936 paper in full, while those wishing to pursue the religious context of a pre-Christian morris should take warning that Celtic religion was taught orally, without written record, and so reliable information is very hard to come by. Tales of the Druids are almost all romantic fiction sparked off by William Stukeley (1687–1765) in his declining years.

The Anglo-Saxons and Danes were rather better documented and an excellent, though gloomy, impression of their religion can be gained from Brian Branston's book, *The Lost Gods of England*, 1957 and 1974.

* * * * *

I have spent some time on the possibilities of a pre-Christian origin for morris because, although this idea is commonly waved about, seldom has any thought been given to the logical consequences. Cecil Sharp was a great enthusiast for the 'primitive religious ceremonial' idea, and for beginnings among 'seasonal pagan observances' with overtones of sacrifice and fertility ritual. Such pictures ought to be incompatible with Christianity, and so the origin of morris was thought to lie among the warm, dark, earthy, pre-Christian days where our ignorance of the prevailing religion enables us to imagine anything we choose. It seems clear that it was Sharp's advocacy of these ideas that won for them a wide popular acceptance; while the romanticism of the inter-war years saw no reason to comment upon the scarcity of supporting facts. But it would be unfair to lay all the blame for this upon Sharp himself, for his explanation obviously struck a resonant chord in the people he knew and they rose more than halfway to meet him. This readiness to accept a mystical origin marks an important aspect of people's attitude towards the morris and this is worthy of a closer look.

Something quite deep inside us is convinced that we live in an ordered world – a world where everything has a place and a purpose. Our pride goes on to assure us that we are quite capable of understanding all these purposes – if only they are properly explained. Say, for example, that we come out of a supermarket and see a group of people doing something strange on the pavement. The mind claws for an explanation. Are they making a film? Are they students raising money for charity? Are they mad? Am I mad? Some solve the problem by fixing their eyes on the ground at their feet and walking by without seeing. Others come out from the crowd and demand, with an urgency rather greater than the situation seems to warrant, "Who are you? Where d'you come from? What's it all for?" We need an explanation: for without one we are uneasy, as we are with things that go bump in the night.

The great thing about this idea of morris growing out of some pre-Christian ritual is that it holds seeds enough to suit all levels of enquiry. For the casual tourist it means, simply, a quaint old English custom. For a more attentive observer the explanation suggests living links with a remote past, together with a feeling that there is something more to the dance than ordinary entertainment. Those of a romantic turn of thought could ramble where the Dark Ages blend into fairy tale, and the serious student could see beginnings in real historical time – but time at an immemorial distance. Faced with such an excellent explanation it seems churlish to aim deliberately at its Achilles heel and say, 'But is it true?' Alas, I fear the answer must be 'No', for I cannot believe that all the people who wrote about morris before Sharp's time (not forgetting the Puritans) could have missed such an important point. However, I do not want this negative answer to wipe out the element of mystery that is such an important ingredient of morris. All I wish to call in doubt is whether this mystery should be equated with what we normally call religion – be it Christian, or pre-Christian, or Moorish.

Allow me to offer a slightly different interpretation of the word *morris*: an interpretation that is no more than a minor adjustment to Rodney Gallop's work, but one that gets us away from the religious implications. He took four examples from the Portuguese language.

	Literal meaning	*Colloquial meaning*
'mouro'	Moor	A new-born child before baptism.
'mouras'	Moorish women	Sprites or fairies.
'antas de mouros'	Caves of the Moors	Megalithic chamber tombs.
'coisas de mouros'	Things of the Moors	Archaeological remains, sherds, etc.

He suggested from this evidence that the moorish element was used to denote something pre-Christian or pagan. I want to modify that idea slightly and suggest that it was used with the sense of 'something from an earlier people'; 'something from the mists of elder days'; 'an explanation for things with origins not granted us to understand'. Or, put more simply, something from a long time ago. It is easy to fit this meaning to chamber tombs and sherds and it isn't too difficult to think of fairies in the same sort of way, but a new-born child? Take a dispassionate look into the eyes of a baby during its first three days of life, before it tunes into our surroundings – there is a strangeness; an other-worldness; a look that has led some Christian communities to seek baptism as a matter of urgency.

To follow this hypothesis further it is convenient to draw together the ideas I have offered into a single word. Although not ideal, the most appropriate seems to be the adjective 'traditional', and I must ask readers to bear in mind the fuller sense for which the word 'traditional' stands symbol when I say that a 'moorish' dance means a 'traditional' dance. The logic of this proposal requires the Moors to be a distant memory before a dance can be called morisco; so if we take 1085 (when the Moors were driven from Toledo) as a key date for the Moorish departure, then the first mention of an event that sounds like a morisco, in 1137, fits the theory in a most satisfying way. It is such a pity that the 1137 reference is almost certainly spurious. If we take a more likely date for the first mention of morisco, say somewhere around 1440, the Moors were then a small and fading enclave far away in southern Spain, so perhaps my proposal can still fit the case.

Both Rodney Gallop and Violet Alford had considerable difficulty with the dance material they found in Spain and Portugal because the term *morisco* was used to describe such a very wide variety of events. They were disappointed at being unable to identify even one characteristic element that was common to all the morisco performances that they had seen. Our current line of thinking resolves the problem: for if we substitute 'traditional' for 'morisco', then the situation becomes clear – a dance in one place may be called traditional, while a different dance in another place may also be called traditional (as may a play, or a style of basket making), without placing any requirement upon us to find links between them, other than their traditionalness. If links do exist, then they are more likely to lie behind the dances, tying them back into a traditional past, rather than appearing crossways to a geographical survey.

What new light now shines on the morris in England? Morris dance is the anglicised form of the word *morisco*, and so we may take it that morris dance also means traditional. This provides an immediate explanation as to how dances as diverse as Cotswold, Northwest and Longsword may all be called morris. It also warns us to treat with caution the theory that claims Cotswold developed out of Longsword. A third result flowing from this new idea is the shedding of some light onto an oddity of the folk world – the fact that some performers of mumming plays were called morris dancers, even when their play contained no dance (traditional play:–morisco:–morris dance).

A little speculation on the position so far: from the fifteenth century onward, Spain and Portugal used 'morisco' to mean 'traditional' and the word with its colloquial meaning travelled to England. Once here, we may think of the word attaching itself to an English dance custom that was old enough to be called traditional, but not so old that it had a firmly established name of its own. The Wetenhale will makes it clear that 'moreys dauns' was understood in England by 1458 and so, perhaps, we might conclude that the very first English morris dance took place not much more than a generation before this date – just to toss in a figure, how about 1430?

I have suggested that the words *morisco* and *morris* both carry with them a sense of obscure beginnings, and this has an unfortunate consequence, for it points to a paradox in the phrase, 'a history of morris'. How can a history deal with something whose beginnings are, by definition, obscure? I offer no answer to this problem; I merely pass on the observation that many dancers seem to prefer origins that retain a covering of cloud. To such people I offer a sincere apology.

APPENDIX TO CHAPTER 4
A morris concordance

Any study of early morris soon uncovers a substantial gathering of words which swirl around the ideas of Moor, morris and morisco. Even if we put aside the fanciful spellings, we are still left with a sizeable family of words with meanings, or hints at meanings, that have been manipulated by authors with varying degrees of linguistic skill and used to colour theories of morris evolution. In my view this is a field in which to avoid dogmatism, so I have collected together this concordance, deliberately ignoring alphabetical order, so that it may be read through in the spirit of a psychologist's word association exercise – not as a dictionary.

MOOR	Someone from Morocco or thereabouts. A follower of Islam.
BLACKAMOOR	Someone with a dark skin.
MOORISH	Something from the land of the Moors or from the time of the Moors.
MORISCO	Spanish for 'Moorish'.
MOORISKE DANS	Flemish – noted by the Oxford Dictionary as perhaps the immediate source for 'morris-dance'.
LA MORISQUE	The word used by Arbeau.
MORISCO	A Moor in Spain. More specifically, either a Moor living under Christian rule, or someone of Moorish origin converted to Christianity.
MORISCO	Traditional dance performance in Spain or Portugal. These performances vary widely in content and style.
MORISCA	A grotesque dance of young men about a woman, usually seen in engravings of the sixteenth century. A fool's dance, or 'Ring Morris'.
MORESQUE	A kind of grotesque painting (Douce).
MARISCO TAVERN	The only pub on the island of Lundy. Named after the Norman family, one of whom, William de Marisco, in 1242, was the first man to be hung, drawn and quartered. Research has so far failed to link this event to morris.
MORRIS	Slang: "To hang dangling in the air, to be executed" (*New Canting Dictionary*, 1725).
MOURISCA	Portuguese for an open-air pantomime.

MOURISCADAS	Dramatic dance from the Azores.
MORISMA	'A multitude of Moors'. Also the name for a Moor and Christian battle/play/dance at Ainsa in Spain.
MORESQUE	Dance/mime of a battle between Moors and Christians (sometimes Turks or Saracens deputise for the Moors). Customs of this sort were widespread under a variety of different spellings and some of them survive to the present day (for example, the Moreska at Korčula in Croatia). The phrase, 'haber moros y cristianos' is said to be used in Spain meaning 'to have a great dispute'.
MATACHINS	Dance/mime of a fight. Probably unrelated to moresque but often confused with it. The character of a matachins seems to lie in the stylistic gestures of the individuals taking part, whereas a moresque is more like a mass attack.
PYRRHICA SALTATIO	A dance by the Roman priests of Mars. Essential equipment seems to have included gilt-paper helmets and bells on the legs. Clashing noises and martial gestures were made with sword and shield.
BUFFONS	From the old French *bouffons*, a sword dance, and very close to *bouffon*, a fool (or buffoon). The dances called buffons, pyrrhic and matachins all seem very similar.

Taille haulte

Reuers bas

Sketches of buffons by Arbeau.

SWORD DANCE	Sword dances are still to be seen in Britain today: in the north-east there are the linked circle dances, Longsword and Rapper, while in Scotland there is step dance over sword and scabbard laid on the ground. These seem to have no connection at all with the matachins type of dance. The only recent representation of a matachins I have seen was on a calendar from China.
CHIRONOMIA	A dance with emphasis on hand gestures. In 1567, Junius translated 'chironomus juvenali' as 'danseur de morisques'.
DYSARD	Fool (dizzard first recorded 1529): related to 'dizzy'.
BAVIAN	May be a baboon, or someone making grimaces: a fool; an attendant character.
MOWREN	Someone of Moorish appearance taking the role of fool, or attendant character.
MORION	Helmet or cap.
MAY MORIAN	Might be a boy with a decorated cap attendant upon morris dancers in May (see Bount, 1656).
MARIAN	Name supposedly given to a young girl appointed May Queen, with the sense of 'Little Virgin Mary'.
MAY MARIAN	In some sources the word 'may' seems to be an abbreviation of 'maid' and carry the sense of 'virgin'.

> 'A bed, a bed,' Clerk Saunders said,
> 'A bed for you and me!'
> 'Fye na, fye na,' said may Margaret,
> 'Till anes we married be!'

MAY	It is often difficult to be sure whether this word refers to the month, to the flower, or to the innocent quality of a young woman. A festival held in early summer was often called a 'May', whether the calendar agreed or not, and certainly there were people who danced round maypoles in June.[1] Elizabeth I was well known as the Virgin Queen – did this idea translate into country custom as the May Queen?

[1] A churchwarden account book for Northill, Bedfordshire, listed expenditure "Layd out for the maye which was the 10 of June 1565".

MAID MARIAN	A French import of circa 1500 from an idyllic and pastoral background, who became a sexless companion for Robin Hood.
MAID MARIAN	"A pricker, a prancer, a tearer of sheets" – the Friar's wench. Presumably this is the French import after contact with the English.[1]
MAYMARRION	A man dressed as a woman. Denounced by Fetherston the Puritan. There is some evidence for a May morning custom where men and women went into the woods and swapped clothes!
MORES	"Customs or conventions regarded as essential to a social group" (OED.)
MORRIS-DANCE	"A grotesque dance performed by persons in fancy costume, usually representing characters from the Robin Hood legend, esp. Maid Marian and Friar Tuck." So says the *Oxford English Dictionary*! It is surprising that such a highly respected source should be so thoroughly wrong. The word *grotesque* is usually applied to illustrations of the sixteenth-century fool's dance which may or may not be an early form of morris. The Robin Hood characters certainly appeared in May Games, but there is no evidence for them ever taking part in the dance (see Douce, 1807).[2] The OED may like to consider the following definition for their next edition: 'Traditional English dances of ceremonial or display character which may be grouped according to the localities from which they were collected (Cotswold, Lancashire, etc.).'
MORRIS-PIKE	A form of pike supposed to have Moorish origins; first recorded in 1487. Barbara Lowe notes a processional giant called 'Lord Marlingspikes' or 'Marespykes', in 1521.
NINE MEN'S MORRIS	A board game, or an outdoor game played with black stone markers and holes cut in the turf. No connection with dancing.

[1] From a play of Robin Hood printed by Copland in the 1550s: see Barbara Lowe, 1955.
[2] Apart from the professionally organised pageants of Victorian times in which many flights of fancy were presented under the banner of 'Merrie England'.

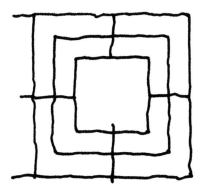

A 'board' for Nine Men's Morris as scratched onto a fourteenth-century stone coffin at Sandwell Priory, West Bromwich (*Current Archaeology*, No. 113).

MERILS	'A play among boys, otherwise call'd Fivepenny Morris' (1706).
MAURICE	English personal name from the Latin 'Mauritius', meaning 'Moorish'. P.H. Reaney's *Dictionary of British Surnames* includes: Mauricius 1176 Richard Maurice 1252
MORIS	First recorded as an English personal name in 1346.
MORIARTY	Anglicised form of the Irish name 'Moriertagh' (meaning 'sea warrior'). Sometimes further anglicised to 'Morris'. Those with a taste for red herring might like to argue that the word 'Viking' also means 'sea warrior' and so 'morris' could mean a Norwegian dance come by way of Ireland.
MOR-UASAL	Celtic words meaning 'great' and 'noble'. Offered as a root for morris in a Glossary by Dr Mackay, 1887, and accepted by Mary Neal.
MORRIUS	King of Veii, possible founder of the Salii, the dancing warrior-priests of Mars who were noted for high jumps (Sir James Frazer).
MARUTS	"A band of dancing warriors attendant upon Indra." This was noted by Mary Neal (*English Folk-Song and Dance*, 1915) from A. Kuhn and deserves a prize as the most unlikely source ever offered for the word *morris*.

MOLLY DANCE	Possibly a regional variation of 'morris dance', although the dance does include a man in woman's clothing called a 'Molly'. It is just possible that this character was introduced to account for an otherwise inexplicable name.
MERRY DANCERS	Thought by some to mean the same as the 'dance of fools', which might be the same as the dance in the Feast of Fools that Strutt believed to be the origin of morris.
MERRY DANCE	Could be another regional variation of 'morris dance'. There is an unclear reference to 'Three Merry Dancers of Wales'. Compare 'Robin Hood and his Merry Men' – for Robin Hood, in the May Game, often had morris dancers among his attendants. Before Robin there was 'Holly and his Merry Men' – another forest sprite in earlier guise. Holly seems to have competed with 'Ivy and her Maidens', which makes one wonder whether 'The Holly and the Ivy' is as innocent a story as the Christmas carol would have us believe.

The list cannot be complete, but it is sufficient to illustrate the minefield we have chosen to explore.

CHAPTER 5

SETTING THE STAGE

The Norman success of 1066 left England with a split down the middle. On one side were the powerful Norman land-owning nobles speaking Norman French and isolated by the protection of great houses: on the other side were the native communities speaking Middle English and leading a rural life in close contact with the land and its traditions. This gap persisted for something like two hundred and eighty years until, as we have already seen, the longbow and the Black Death moved the point of balance and the gap began to close. I am now going to suggest that it was the closing of this social gap which provided the conditions that started drama into growth; and since it is in among these early forms of drama that we get our first sight of morris dancers, it is a development we ought to know something about.

Landowners in the middle of the fourteenth century were faced with problems. The population had been cut back by plague; so labour was now scarce and the price had gone up. Put another way, the labourer had increased in his value and what was certainly true in the economic sphere was probably also true in the social sense as well. The longbow had become the dominant weapon in battle and so the power to defend the realm had fallen into the hands of villagers. A lord, called upon by his King to raise an army, now had no option but to consider the physical fitness, skill-at-arms and goodwill of the villagers on his estate. Given this situation, we can reasonably deduce that the villager rose, in the eyes of his lord, from being little more than a farm animal to being a fellow human being and perhaps, in some circumstances, even a friend. "Once more unto the breach, dear friends" – Shakespeare's words in the mouth of Henry V are unreliable history, but they bring to our minds the new relationship that might now be possible between the rich and the ordinary. This closing of the gap and the re-establishment of human contact between the high and the low in society formed the soil within which the customs and traditions of village life could be fertilised by the money, spare time and facilities of the lord's house. Out of this soil grew drama.

I have, no doubt, irritated most historians by pinning the whole of this social process onto just two events: the battle of Crécy, 1346, and the Black Death, 1349, and I accept that this is an oversimplification. Nevertheless, these markers draw our attention to the middle of the fourteenth century;

to the place where accounts of dramatic activity suddenly start to appear. The middle of the fourteenth century is also right in the middle of Edward III's reign – when Francis Peck supposed that morris was introduced into England.[1]

What, then, were these customs and traditions of village life that existed before my hypothetical start-date of 1350? What were the games and pastimes which formed the clay out of which early drama was moulded? Regrettably, and for reasons already discussed at length, the sum total of historical evidence available to help us at this point is very small. Enid Welsford in *The Court Masque* has suggested three types of early traditional game, although there is very little to support or deny her ideas.

1) The King Game – carrying with it ideas of mock ruler; a lord of misrule; perhaps a lay equivalent of the elected abbot or pope in the Feast of Fools.
2) The Sword Dance – a stylish mime of combat; a matachins.
3) Mummers – a procession of disguised people; the ancestors of those who appear later in this chapter.

One of the rare clues to come down to us from this very early period is recorded in the Synod of Worcester (1240), where a strict command was given.

Do not be present at sinful pastimes; do not support games for the making of King and Queen or for the raising of Rams; and do not support public wrestling.
(From the Latin of Brand, 1841, translation by Mark West, 1983)

What I have said so far has ignored one important strand of the story. Religious plays seem to have grown up in a rather different atmosphere from the secular pastimes presumably because they drew funds and respectability straight from the Church itself and the actors avoided the disreputable image that followed most other performers of the time. Church drama had outgrown the church building and moved out onto the street some three generations earlier than my key date of 1350 – round about the time when the feast of Corpus Christi was invented in 1265. (Set a couple of months after Easter, Corpus Christi was well placed, climatically, for outdoor celebration, and processions were frequently a feature of the day.)

[1.] There is some danger of circular logic if we look upon this as confirmatory evidence, because Peck may simply have been aware of the emergence of drama around this time, and assumed that morris was a part of it.

70

We can now move on and, as it were, pass the starting post and get into the field where there is some tangible evidence. This field might reasonably be described as 'late mediaeval' and I take it to stretch for 165 years, from the earliest item on my list in 1347, up to the point in 1512 where Renaissance influences from Italy caused a substantial change of direction. Several long and careful studies of this period have already been published: *Annals of the Stage* (1831) by J. Payne Collier; *The Mediaeval Stage* (1903) by Sir E.K. Chambers[1] and *The Court Masque* (1927) by Enid Welsford. I, for my part, intend no more than a light skip across the quicksand.

To start with, we have something of a problem with terminology. Masque and mascarade, ludus, mumming and momerie – these and many other names circulate without any consistency of definition. The names relate, more or less loosely, to styles of performance that were themselves changing with the fashion of passing years, while the whim of performers knew no fixed rules. Add to this a confusion of new ideas and yet more names flooding in from the courts of continental Europe; remind ourselves that mediaeval chroniclers were probably quite casual in the way they matched name to performance; and then we can see why the three books mentioned above are a bit short on clarity.

It will not, by now, surprise any of us to discover that the great majority of early references tell of events that were set firmly within the context of court life. It is also worth a reminder that communications between Court and Court would have been fairly good, in spite of the distances, and that ideas, particularly ideas about fashion, would have spread internationally, at court level, far more speedily than more mundane thoughts would flow from village to nearby village.

In an attempt to bring order to this complex and shadowy world I propose to marshal the material under eight separate headings. This is no more than a device to aid clarity and must not be taken to imply eight watertight compartments, for ideas drift and merge and there is a spider's web of interconnections. My subject is, of course, morris, and the reason for this present study of drama is to describe the stage upon which, in due course, morris will make its entrance. It might therefore happen that events of critical importance to the development of drama, but of little relevance to morris, may get less than a fair showing. My central theme will also give the following account a slant in favour of the English material, which would not be justifiable in a work more generally based.

[1.] In his preface, Chambers refers to Collier as "This slovenly and dishonest antiquary".

1. Religious Plays

As already indicated, religious plays were first in the field and so we may presume that they had some influence on the many forms of drama that came along later. The texts of a number of these plays have survived and studies have been made on their theological content (for example, much careful thought has been expended on the precise meaning of the word 'mystery', first used to describe a play in 1402), but these are aspects which have little to do with morris: more important from our point of view is the way in which the plays were presented. It is not entirely clear whether the Corpus Christi celebration introduced the idea of a festive procession, or whether the Church simply took over a pre-existing custom, but in either case there is little doubt that the procession came to be an important feature of mediaeval life. There seem to have been two variations on the processional theme: either the exhibits passed by a stationary audience; or the audience processed past stationary exhibits. The first required any set-piece drama to be presented on a mobile stage, while the second required a temporary stage to be erected at the roadside. A wheeled or temporary stage to suit these requirements was called a 'pageant': a word which later transferred from the stage itself to the performance on that stage.

2. Entremets

This word of French or Burgundian origin carries the sense of 'something inserted'; 'something special introduced as a pleasant diversion'; 'an interlude'; and for most of the period we are currently considering, the thing into which the entremet was inserted was a banquet. The entremet itself started off as being an unusual dish of food – a tour de force by the cooks – but as time went on the spectacular effect became all-important and the edible requirement faded away. Pies became no more than a concealment for surprises. Then all reference to food was left behind and the entremet became a conversation-piece: a wonder for the diversion of the guests. The pursuit of novelty and opulent display then required the changing of entremets during the course of a banquet, and the need for mobility turned the entremet into a pageant. The word 'entremet' was not used in England: here, the earlier forms were known as a 'subtilty' and the later ones as a 'disguising'.

A well-known nursery rhyme tells us of

> Four and twenty blackbirds baked in a pie.
> When the pie was opened, the birds began to sing.
> Wasn't that a dainty dish to set before a king.

And there is little doubt that pies of this sort were actually prepared. All one needs to understand is the simple trick of baking the piecrust over a temporary support and then inserting the birds through a concealed opening when the pie was cold. That sounds fairly straightforward, but our sense of wonder must surely be stirred, even today, by the thought of the practical problems of assembling the entremets that were described for a great banquet given by Philip, Duke of Burgundy, on 18th February 1454.

> In this hall there were three tables loaded with the most elaborate entremets, the first of which was a glass church, very prettily made, it had a sounding bell and four singers inside it who were to sing and play upon the organ. There was a naked boy on a rock pissing rosewater; there was a gibbet; and at another table there was a pie that contained twenty-eight living people who played on musical instruments, each as his turn came. There was a man beating a bush filled with little birds, and nearby an orchard surrounded by rose trellises in which a knight and a lady were seated at a table eating fledglings: the man beating the bush was indicating to the lady with his thumb that he was labouring in vain and wasting his time. [One assumes this must have been a model illustrating some well-known story or saying.] In the middle of the hall was a high pillar on which was raised the statue of a naked woman with her blonde hair hanging down behind. She wore a rich headdress and was draped in a veil worked with greek letters and from her right breast poured hippocras for as long as the feast lasted. Nearby a fine living lion was chained to a shorter pillar which carried the inscription in letters of gold, 'Do not touch my lady'. Once the meal had started, mobile exhibits came in – a monster with the legs and feet of a gryphon and a man doing a handstand on its shoulders; a horse entered backwards bearing two masked trumpeters who sat back to back as they sounded a fanfare ....
> [And so this bizarre entertainment proceeded on its curious way.] [1]

Another Burgundian example from 1468 has a great golden lion covered with the arms of Burgundy carrying on his back the female dwarf of Madame of Burgundy, dressed as a shepherdess. The lion sang a song and the shepherdess was placed on the table and received very humanely by Madame. "For the next entremets there was a dromedary." [2]

For sheer scale, it is difficult to beat "the arrival of two giants who entered the hall armed with staves dragging after them a great whale sixty

---

[1.] A selection from the many items recorded in voluminous detail in the Chronicles of Mathieu de Coussy, 1444–1461; Ed. Buchon, 1838, translation by Kitty Vernon, 1984.
[2.] Wedding of Charles the Bold at Bruges. Olivier de La Marche, quoted in Welsford.

feet long, moving his fins and body and tail as if alive". The whale moved round the hall before disgorging sirens, followed in due course by a dozen knights of the sea who "jumped out one after the other in a moresque" [forty people travelled in the stomach of this whale!].[1] Even allowing for a bit of exaggeration it is difficult to imagine a mediaeval hall crowded with guests and tables that still had enough space to turn a sixty-foot whale. (Mediaeval halls were long and narrow, with the width defined by the timber available for roofing. Westminster Hall, built 1399, is quite exceptionally wide at 68 feet.) I would have expected trouble with the doorways as well.

3. Lords of Misrule

The Lord of Misrule seems to have been an English speciality, although Scotland had a very similar official who was often called the Abbot of Unreason. The 'Lord' was a master of ceremonies and leader of the junketings that commonly took place round about Christmas time, and may well have been a secular equivalent or successor to the Pope of Fools who was once elected by minor clergy to lead the mock-religious celebration known as the Feast of Fools, or December Liberties. In 1391 the Archbishop of York issued an injunction to the Provost of Beverley Minster "that he abolish the corrupt and ancient custom of the King of Fools, both within the church and without". These names all have a loud anti-establishment ring to them, and we may deduce that a limited period of folly and licence in the dark days of winter was a necessary antidote to a life hedged-in by hard work, hunger, cold, disease and early death.

An early puff of Puritan thought towards the middle of the sixteenth century caused these colourful, noisy and mediaeval Lords of Misrule to lose official favour, and the task of getting up entertainments moved over to a seemingly more respectable officer, the Master of the Revels. 'The Revels' is a term that came to be used of entertainment in a fairly general sense, but the early French origins of the word point strongly to rebellion and revolution, so Revel and Misrule both look to a world turned upside down.

Besides having an organisational function, some Lords of Misrule would draw popular fun from the timeless theme of a servant suddenly elevated to a position of authority, where he may parody the behaviour of those more normally in that position. I am reminded of my father's stories of army life in the 1930s when, at Christmas time, the youngest recruit was allowed to write out the orders for the day.

[1] More from the wedding of Charles the Bold.

4. Civic Processions

It has always been advisable for Kings and Princes, and Queens as well, to be seen and recognised by the people they rule. In days before television and photography, one of the most effective ways of being seen by the multitude was to ride in a formal procession, for most of the townspeople could be relied upon to leave their jobs and line the streets so that they could wonder at the finery of the nobles and gaze at the sideshows arranged along the route. A King's return to his capital was frequently cause for a procession of this sort, and it is easy to think of good political reasons why this should be so. Enid Welsford quotes from Jehan Froissart, who was eye-witness to an event of this kind.

On Sunday the 20th of August 1389 when Isabella, Queen of France, arrived in Paris, pageants and tableaux had been arranged at all the more prominent parts of the city through which she was to pass. At the first gate of St Denis there was a starry heaven with a golden sun radiating light (the symbolical device of the King) and full of children dressed as angels who sang sweetly; there was also an image of the Madonna and Child.

Round the fountain of St Denis young girls sang sweetly as they offered wine to all the passers-by. A little further on a stage was erected in the street on which was performed a combat between Christians and Saracens.[1] At the second gate of St Denis, God the Holy Trinity was seated in majesty surrounded by choir-boys dressed as angels and as the Queen passed by, the gate of Paradise opened and two singing angels placed a golden crown upon her head.

At the gate of the Chatelet of Paris there was a wooden castle on which was a bed curtained and adorned as though for the King's chamber. This bed was called the 'Bed of Justice' and in it lay the figure of St Anne. The castle also contained quite a large enclosure full of trees with birds and hares and conies flying and running in and out. From this thicket there issued a white stag who approached the Bed of Justice, while from the other side of the thicket came a lion and an eagle, very well made, who proudly walked up to the stag and the Bed of Justice. At this, twelve young girls holding naked swords in their hands came out of the wood and put themselves in position to protect the stag and the Bed of Justice.

The first part of Froissart's account might be described as simple symbolism, but the Bed of Justice sequence is an early move towards a

---

[1.] We will see this fight again and in rather more detail in Chapter 6.

rather more complex allegory. As ideas became more subtle and abstract, so words took on a more important share in these presentations. Thus, when the ten-year-old King Henry VI returned from France in February 1432 and entered London:

> The King found on the drawbridge a goodly tower out of which issued Dame Nature, Dame Grace and Dame Fortune, all of whom addressed to him poetical speeches. At the right hand of these three ladies stood seven virgins who presented the King with the seven gifts of the Holy Ghost; and on the left hand were another seven virgins who gave him the seven gifts of Grace. After this salutation they sang a round with a heavenly melody. [The speeches were probably written by John Lydgate.]
>
> At the entry of Cornhill there was ordained a tabernacle of curious work in the which stood Dame Sapience and about her the seven arts or liberal sciences. As first grammar, logic, rhetoric, music, arithmetic, geometry and astronomy; every each of them exercising their cunning and faculty.
>
> At the conduit in Cornhill there was set a pageant made circle-wise and in the summit or top thereof was set a child of wonderful beauty, apparelled like a king, upon whose right hand sat Lady Mercy and upon the left hand Lady Truth and over them stood Dame Cleanness embracing the king's throne. Then before the king stood two judges and eight sergeants of the coif; and Dame Cleanness had this speech to Henry the King ...
>
> At the conduit in Cheap were ordained a number of wells – as the Well of Mercy, the Well of Grace and the Well of Pity; and at every well a lady standing, that ministered the water of every well to such as would ask it, and that water was turned into good wine. About these wells were also set a variety of trees with flourishing leaves and fruits – the which were so cunningly wrought that to many they appeared natural trees growing.
>
> A little further on there was a wonderful tower and artificial trees which showed the title of Henry to the crown of France.[1]

Items in a procession are always rather miscellaneous in character but there are a few points of general interest to be seen in these mediaeval examples before we move on. Many of the ideas obviously derive from the Church, but they are Church teachings at some considerable remove from the pulpit. The religious plays had taken spiritual and moral lessons from

---

[1] Extracted from a long and flowery account by Robert Fabyan, Alderman of Farringdon Without (died 1512), in *The New Chronicles of England and France*, published 1516 and 1811.

the Church and turned them into a popular dramatic form, and we may presume that it was these dramatic forms that were then further remodelled and used to press the political point and purpose that lay behind a particular procession. Surrounded as we are today with the media and the printed word, it is difficult for us to appreciate the impact that these dramatic pictures and symbols would have had among a community that was untravelled and totally illiterate. Another influence on the mediaeval procession came, no doubt, through the hands of the builders who used their skill and imagination to construct the settings of these elaborate tableaux – men, we must assume, from the local craft guilds, with the occasional woman as unofficial helper. Finally, we can see here the mediaeval use of a technique well-known to every modern advertising executive – pretty girls and free alcohol.

The period we are examining, from 1347 to 1512, was selected to match up with a distinct phase in the growth of dramatic activity, but this same span of years covers other parallel changes which also have a bearing on our study: better boats led to more trade and so to the founding of merchant communities in the major ports, while craft guilds grew to become an important element in town life. Here we see the development of a specialist society and the start of a middle class. In London, at least, people from this new class took a prominent part in processions.

5. Tournaments

Heavily armed and armoured men on sturdy horses first came to dominate a battlefield at Hastings, against Harold, and in those days, we should remind ourselves, a knight could be seen as a tenant paying his rent with war service on horseback.

The first tournaments, we may guess, were introduced to encourage skill-at-arms and thereby improve military potential, so an early tournament resembled war rather than sport. But by 1350, knighthood had taken on a religious and mystical significance and rules had been introduced to make the tournaments a bit safer. Indeed, we can see something of a balancing transition: as the knights declined in importance on the battlefield, pushed out first by pike, and then by longbow and finally by firearms, so they became more involved with the institutions of chivalry and the pageantry of tournament. Through the fourteenth and fifteenth centuries tournaments were enormously popular with young men, and some not so young, ranging from Sweden to Portugal, seeking adventures and increasing their fame, or, put into modern language, trying to win prizes at tournaments.

The element of disguise runs strongly through many of these mediaeval pastimes and the tournament was no exception: we read of the King and Court riding to the lists masked as Tartars, or again, in 1343, that the knights jousted in Smithfield disguised as the Pope and the twelve Cardinals (Chambers). In 1375 we hear of that particularly nasty piece of work, Alice Perrers, riding as Lady of the Sun from the Tower of London through Cheap, as a prelude to the great jousts in Smithfield (Chambers). When Charles the Bold married Margaret of York in 1468 the chief entertainment was a magnificent six-day tournament.

> On one day the Count of Roussy came on horseback enclosed in a four-towered castle with a great door that could shut and open of itself. He despatched his dwarf 'Petit Espoir' to plead for his freedom. When the ladies gave orders for his release the door of the castle opened and the knight on his horse leapt out and entered the lists.
> (Olivier de la Marche, in Welsford.)

An audience in the mood to enjoy itself, gathered for a tournament, would naturally attract all sorts of other entertainers.

6. Disguisings

A disguising was the development in England of an idea known on the Continent as the entremets, and under this latter heading we have already seen something of the wonders and curiosities that were introduced into Burgundian banqueting-halls. A feature of the show that took on a special importance in England was the decoration of the pageant with groups of disguised people, and this led to the whole performance being called a disguising. In spite of the name, concealment of individual identity seems to have been of no great consequence (unlike in mumming and the early sixteenth-century masques, where true disguise was essential). Presumably the disguisers were paid entertainers and the clothes for a disguising were primarily intended as theatrical costume.

The use of groups of people in 'sets', each set being all of the same sex and similarly disguised, may have been a mediaeval technique for amplifying the image. This idea of sets is well illustrated by the earliest disguising noted by Enid Welsford. In 1347 King Edward III held Christmas at Guildford and his wardrobe roll lists a substantial number of properties that came in sets of fourteen. There were forty-two visors, fourteen with faces of women, fourteen with faces of bearded men and fourteen with silver heads of angels; there were fourteen cloaks depicting dragon's heads; fourteen tunics with head and wings of peacocks; fourteen tunics with head and wings of swans, and so on (from the Latin of Chambers). Our

78

knowledge is, as usual, limited by the nature of the source, and wardrobe accounts have nothing to tell us about what the performers did in these costumes, but Strutt's plate XVI gives some idea of what they must have looked like.

Strutt found this illustration in *The Romance of Alexander*,
a manuscript of 1344 (see Chapter 8).

It might be irrelevant, but I am reminded of the Christmas carol that runs,

> Twelve drummers drumming;
> Eleven pipers piping;
> Ten lords a-leaping;
> Nine ladies dancing;
> Eight maids a-milking;
> Seven swans a-swimming; et cetera.

The ending of the Wars of the Roses (1485) brought a general relief which sparked an upturn in entertainment: pageants became more elaborate and the drama and dance components took on a more important position. The marriage of Henry VII's heir, Prince Arthur, to Catherine of Aragon in 1501 introduced a level of splendour to the English Court that had not been seen for a very long time. A passage from one of the accounts tells of a disguising.

The King caused Westminster Hall to be adorned with rich hangings and a huge cupboard of plate. On Friday evening when all the court was assembled there entered a 'most goodly and pleasant disguising conveyed and showed in pageants proper and subtle'. A wonderfully devised castle

was drawn into the hall by four great artificial animals. Eight disguised ladies were looking out of the windows of the castle and on each of the four turrets sat a little boy, dressed like a maiden, who sang sweetly as the pageant advanced into the hall. The next event was the arrival of a lady dressed like a Spanish Princess who came in on a ship that appeared to be sailing upon the sea, the ship's captain and crew speaking and behaving in nautical fashion. They cast anchor near the castle and two goodly persons called Hope and Desire descended by a ladder, approached the castle and informed the ladies that they were ambassadors from certain Knights of the Mount of Love who wished to come and court them. The ladies, however, 'gave their small answer of utterly refuse' and while the ambassadors were warning them of the grave consequences of their stubbornness, in came the third pageant, which was shaped like a mountain and contained eight goodly knights. As soon as the newcomers had been informed that negotiations had failed, they made a vigorous attack on the castle, reduced it to submission, and induced the ladies to descend into the hall and dance with them.
(Harleian Ms 69, in Welsford.)

Another item from the same occasion tells of two pageants:

the first of which was shaped like an arbour and contained twelve knights who descended and danced many different dances and then stood aside. Then the trumpets blew and in came a pageant 'made round after the fashion of a Lanthorne' with many windows and more than a hundred great lights and all made so transparent that the twelve 'goodly Ladyes disguised' could be clearly seen. These ladies came out and danced alone and then coupled with the knights.
(Welsford.)

7. Mumming

Mumming is by far the most mysterious and difficult of these headings. Enid Welsford has suggested that mumming was a component in the primaeval village pastimes, while those who are familiar with the present-day folk movement will realise that mumming plays are still with us, having emerged out of the mists of folk tradition; but whether or not these are two ends of the same piece of string, we have no sure way of knowing. By great good fortune, a very early and clear description of a mumming has survived and is preserved among the historical manuscripts of the Harleian Collection, it tells of a large procession going mumming to visit Richard II while he was still Prince of Wales, early in 1377. This account makes a convenient starting point for a discussion.

The Comons of London made great sporte and solemnity to the yong prince: for upon the monday next before the purification of our lady [February 2nd] at night and in the night were 130 men disguizedly aparailed and well mounted on horsebacke to goe on mumming to the said prince, riding from Newgate through Cheape whear many people saw them with great noyse of minstralsye, trumpets, cornets and shawmes and great plenty of waxe torches lighted and in the beginning they rid 48 after the maner of esquiers two and two together clothed in cotes and clokes of red say or sendall and their faces covered with vizards well and handsomely made: after these equiers came 48 like knightes well arayed after the same maner: after the knightes came one excellent arrayed and well mounted as he had bene an emperor: after him some 100 yards came one nobly arayed as a pope and after him came 24 arayed like cardinals and after the cardinals came 8 or 10 arayed and with black vizardes like deuils appearing nothing amiable seeming like legates, riding through London and ouer London bridge towards Kenyton wher the yong prince made his aboad with his mother and the D. of Lancaster and the Earles of Cambridge, Hertford Warrick and Suffolk and many other lordes which were with him to hould the solemnity, and when they were come before the mansion they alighted on foot and entered into the haule and soone after, the prince and his mother and the other lordes came out of the chamber into the haule, and the said mummers saluted them, shewing a pair of dice upon a table to play with the prince, which dice were subtilly made that when the prince shold cast he shold winne and the said players and mummers set before the prince three jewels each after other: and first a balle of gould, then a cupp of gould, then a gould ring, the which the said prince wonne at thre castes as before it was appointed, and after that they set before the prince's mother, the D. of Lancaster and the other earles euery one a gould ringe and the mother and the lordes wonne them. And then the prince caused to bring the wyne and they dronk with great joye, commanding the minstrels to play and the trompets began to sound and other instruments to pipe &c. And the prince and the lordes dansed on the onc syde, and the mummers on the other a great while and then they drank and tooke their leaue and so departed toward London.
(Harleian Ms 247, quoted in Chambers.)

Let us have a look at the various elements in this account with the hope that they will guide us to some general understanding of mumming. The procession was clearly an important part – but then, as we have already seen, processions were a common feature in many different sorts of event.

Disguise, or at least fancy dress, was also widespread in late mediaeval times – although we should note that here the sets of knights and esquires, cardinals and devils suggest formality, rather than an attempt at light-hearted carnival dress. They travelled at night, on horseback, with torches and noisy music: clearly they didn't care who saw them, but if it was a public show, why was it at night? When they reached their destination they dismounted and went into the house where the Prince was lodging. Other accounts of mumming emphasise that such entries were unexpected and without invitation, although I find it difficult to believe that a hundred and thirty disguised men would have been allowed entry to the future King's presence without some kind of authority and foreknowledge. What did this great body of men come to do? They came to play dice! Not only that, but they came to play with loaded dice: and, stranger still, their own dice were loaded against themselves.

It is, I think, quite clear in this particular account that the fundamental purpose was the presentation of gifts – but why the dice? I can only suggest that dicing may, at some earlier time, have been used in divination or fortune-telling or, perhaps, in the sense of bargaining with the fates – as we might still talk of 'dicing with death'. In either case we must presume that by 1377 the custom had declined into conventional social ceremony. The phrase 'shewing a pair of dice' gives some support to those who would claim that the mummers did not speak. Other accounts tell that the name of the game played with dice was 'mumchance' and this word also carries with it a hint of silence or secretiveness together with the concept of luck. The occasion ended with wine, music and dancing, which I take to be relaxation after the essential parts of the mumming were done.

The essence of a mumming in the fourteenth century might therefore be described as 'a procession of masked and disguised people in serious mood, who made uninvited entry to houses, where they played dice with the occupants'. We could go on to list another four features which might have been important: silence; the presentation of gifts; the use of loaded dice; and dancing; but I am inclined to think of these (or at least the last three of them) as accretions brought in to adapt the mumming to a particular circumstance.

It would be satisfying to think of these written accounts from the upper classes as a sophistication built up on a popular game; for then we could adopt Enid Welsford's suggestion of mumming as an early village activity, and go on to see it as a form of 'good-luck visiting' with the mummers casting (or fore-casting) a future for each household with their dice, or perhaps, bargaining with the Fates to bring good luck upon the occupants.

All this is speculation. All we know about mumming among the illiterate classes is that laws were enacted to try and stop it.

Think of the intimidating appearance of a troop of disguised and masked mummers marching by night and the threat, real or imagined, that such a band could inspire in the heart of an honest citizen. Think also how happily some criminal groups must have embraced the mumming custom. We might then find some sympathy for the authorities when they attempted to stamp it out. As early as 1334 an order was made in London forbidding people to go about the streets in this manner.

We do forbid .... that any man shall go about at this Feast of Christmas with companions disguised with false faces, or in any other manner, to the houses of the good folks of the City, for playing at dice there.
(Riley, *Memorials*)

In 1418 it was proclaimed

that no manner person, of what estate, degree, or condition that ever he be, during this holy time of Christmas be so hardy in any wise to walk by night in any manner mumming, plays, interludes, or any other disguisings with any feigned beards, painted visors, deformed or coloured visages in any wise, upon pain of imprisonment.
(Riley, *Memorials*)

There has always been an element of uncertainty between what was a disguising and what was a mumming, and the above quotation shares in the confusion: for what it is worth, I would add my own feeling that a 'disguising' was for the benefit of an audience, whereas a 'mumming' was for the benefit of the participants.

As the spoken word became an increasingly important element in many of these entertainments, so writers appeared on the scene: the earliest one we know about is John Lydgate, whose works can be dated around the period 1427 to 1430. It is reasonable to suppose that the scriptwriters of those days worked on commission to tight deadlines and that they felt free to borrow ideas from any of the preceding styles of performance. These borrowed ideas would then have been remoulded to suit current need. If this was so, then the entry of literary effort into early drama must be seen as a major force for mixing up and blending together. This chapter has been based upon the assumption that some system of classification is possible. If this assumption has any validity, then the entry of the professional writer and the consequent pursuit of novelty were already breaking it down by the middle years of the fifteenth century. Taking a more positive view, we could look upon this process as a weaving together of various strands so as to make drama into a rope with hybrid strength.

8. Village Games

Seven of these headings have looked at entertainment mainly through the eyes of the Establishment – the Church, the aristocracy and the new merchant class. Now, under this last one, I want to give a thought to what was going on in the villages: for here, so everyone tells us, is the true home of the morris dancer.

Our first wisp of positive evidence comes in the Worcester quote of 1240 – 'games for the making of King and Queen' (quoted in full earlier in this chapter) – and some small support for this scanty picture is found at the crowning of Robert the Bruce on 27 March 1306, when the title 'Summer King' was mockingly used in the sense of 'an ephemeral character' (Douce). Perhaps the most illuminating of the early descriptions comes from a Latin paper held in the York Registry which appears to be part of a matrimonial law-suit in which someone is trying very hard to establish an alibi. Thomas Hird, in 1469, deposed that:

> The young folk of the village of Wistow used to follow the national tradition by participating in a summer game [ludum estivalem] which was called, in their own tongue, 'Somergame' .... Then, on the previous Sunday, Margaret More was elected by the young folk as 'queen' for the aforementioned game that Sunday. Concerning which it is painstakingly affirmed that the game was held on that Sunday in a certain nearby barn, beside the cemetery of the church, to which Margaret made her way before twelve o'clock, ie midday, and waited without break in the same place from that time until after sunset on the same day sitting upon her throne and ruling as 'queen'. He says, moreover, that he knows this because he was the seneschal and so took the rôle of butler in the game ... And he testifies that when Margaret had come to the barn in which the game was held, which in the vulgar tongue is called a 'Somerhouse', he remained with her hour by hour all the time until after sunset in the company also of the following who were continuing with the game: Thomas Barker (of Wistow) who was at that time 'king' in the same game; Robert Gafare (also of Wistow) and William Dawson who were then acting as soldiers in the game; not to mention many others who, with them, made up a numerous gathering.[1]

[1.] The Latin given in J.S. Purvis, *Tudor Parish Documents of the Diocese of York*, 1948. Translation by Mark West, 1983.

Churchwardens' accounts have survived in surprisingly large numbers from quite early times to give us a glimpse into those aspects of village life that involved the Church in financial profit or expense. The earliest account is a roll from St Michael, Bath, dating from 1349: four more sets begin in the 1300s and fifty more start in the following century. We owe a debt of thanks to those clerical antiquarians who, in the later decades of the nineteenth century, transcribed most of these records into a form accessible for present study (most notably J. Charles Cox).

Church funds have always been gathered from a variety of sources; rents, bequests and tithes are clearly understood but there was another source that was less well recorded. The idea and the act of pilgrimage were strong forces in the mediaeval mind. Indeed, the nearest approach to a health service was to travel to a shrine and pray for a miracle. A multitude of authorised and unauthorised shrines dotted the country and pilgrims came for their spiritual wellbeing; to fulfill a vow; to earn indulgences for their soul, if they had been poaching or sleeping with a neighbour's wife, because their bishop had commanded them to go. No matter what the reason, an essential part of all pilgrimage was the collecting box – income to the clergy and to the Church.

As the fifteenth century drew towards its close, attitudes towards the Church were becoming more critical, and we may suppose these incomes were declining. New ideas were needed and one of these new ideas was to run a Church Ale, where the Church financed and organised the brewing, baking and roasting of ale, bread and meat, then invited the villagers along to a party – for a small charge. With luck a substantial profit was made and transferred into the Church funds. Favourite days for these festivals were Mayday, Whitsun, Midsummer and Dedication Day. The Reverend Dr Cox has suggested that, since mediaeval man was not permitted to labour on feast days, and since it was deemed inadvisable to leave him standing about with idle hands between the obligatory church services, it would have seemed prudent to the Church to provide him with some entertainment and so turn a Holy Day into a holiday. Personally, I am more convinced by the fund-raising explanation.

At this point it is worth remembering the suggestion already made that, starting from 1350, the authorities would have begun to regard village men as potential soldiers. With this as a pivot for their thinking, we may anticipate an interest in the goodwill, patriotic spirit and skill-at-arms of the villagers and expect some official support for festivities like the Church Ale – particularly where an element of weapons-training could be introduced. An Act of Parliament in 1466 directed that all townships were to establish 'butts' at which every man was required to shoot up and down on all Sundays and holy days.

By the end of the fifteenth century the Church Ale had ceased to be an emergency solution to an occasional cash crisis and had become a regular and vital feature of Church income. It had drawn into itself a variety of entertainments and was now commonly called a 'Game' rather than an 'Ale'. Regrettably, not one description, script or programme of these Games has survived, so we have to make what we can of the account book entries.

Morris is first mentioned by churchwardens at Kingston-upon-Thames in 1507 and this, together with the subsequent mentions, will be considered in detail in Chapter 7. However, Dr Cox offers a few entries earlier than this date that are certainly interesting and possibly relevant.

Somewhere between 1445 and 1455 at St Margaret, Southwark, there was 3s 9d received "In dawnsyng mony of the Maydens".

In 1464 at Tavistock, 2d was paid "To Mayers child for dawnsying with the hobye hors".

In 1483 at Croscombe, Somerset, 6s 8d contributed of "The Wyfes dansyng".

In the time of Henry VII at St Edmund, Salisbury, 3s 4d was received for "Whytsontyde dawnsynge".

In 1490 also at St Edmund, Salisbury, 8d was paid to Willm Belrynger for "Clensinge of the Churche at ye Dawnse of Powles." [Could this be maypole dancing inside the church?] Other references suggest that this was a children's dance, although the very substantial expenditure of 13s 7d in the following year for timber, nails and labour in preparation for the Powlis Daunce makes one think it was more than just entertainment for the kids.

References to the purchase of rushes for strewing the floor are frequent, going back as far as 1385 at Tavistock. These are interesting in view of the regular connection that exists in the nineteenth century between Lancashire morris and the custom of bringing rushes to the church.

The Yeovil accounts of 1457 show that $2\frac{1}{2}$ ells of linen cloth were bought for 15d to make two banners to be carried round the fields; 1d was spent on dyeing it; 6d for making up the banners and $2\frac{1}{2}$d for seven wooden rods to carry them in procession. It was common custom at Rogation Tide to go in procession round the paths and fields of the parish seeking a blessing upon the crops and protection from the plague. Morris tours round a village have sometimes been referred to as 'good-luck visiting' and there is an obvious similarity of feel between this sort of morris and the parochial processions; but whether a link ever existed – or whether one grew out of the other – we do not know.

* * * * *

We have now arrived at 1512 and the background for the earliest morris has already been painted, but before we put the Development of Drama to one side, a very brief look at the masque seems like a good idea, because masque was a form of entertainment that made frequent use of morris.

The masque made its first appearance in England in 1512 and the new arrival bore a striking resemblance to the old mumming custom; what made it new and shocking was the element of flirtation that it introduced into court circles. Without warning, a group of men, masked, hooded and in voluminous cloaks, would gatecrash a party. Each would single out a lady from the company and spend the rest of the evening dancing and chatting her up. If and when the time became tactically opportune, the masquer would unmask. This style of masquing followed a fashion set in the Italian city states: a fashion which shows a frivolous side to the Renaissance. Something like twenty years later, a second ripple of Renaissance thought reached English shores and introduced drama in the classical manner, which then met up with the old disguising; new and old fused together and grew into a structured dramatic presentation that was also called masque.

Put into the simplest of terms, the Renaissance was a revival of interest in art and science that took for its model the classical times of ancient Greece and Rome. It started in Italy and spread across western Europe, bringing a degree of uniformity in both thought and fashion to the upper levels of society. Within this general movement, drama came under review, and particular interest was shown in the revival of classical comedies.[1] From the very beginning there were problems in making the classics palatable to a modern audience and so, to sugar the pill, plays were cut up into short lengths and the spaces between filled with spectacular interludes. These interludes, which had absolutely nothing to do with the play, followed a principle already well established by the entremets and the disguisings. A favourite item in the Italian interludes (or intermezzi) was the morisco.

What do we know of these early Italian performances? In 1491, in a performance of the *Menaechmi*[2] at Ferrara, "There were three very beautiful intermezzi: in the first one a morisco was made carrying torches in their hands ...." In 1501 a dynastic marriage was celebrated between Alphonso, eldest son of the Duke of Ferrara, and Lucrezia Borgia, daughter of the Pope, and then:

---

[1] Production of these plays started at Ferrara in the 1480s.
[2] The play that was developed by Shakespeare into the *Comedy of Errors*.

On New Year's Day [1502] triumphs of various heroes of antiquity were performed in the streets of Rome and comedies were acted in the Vatican. A morisco was performed in the Pope's chamber upon a stage decorated with foliage and lighted by torches. After a short eclogue, a jongleur dressed as a woman danced the morisco to the accompaniment of tambourines; Cesare Borgia himself took part in the performance and was recognised in spite of his disguise. Trumpets announced a second performance – a tree appeared with a Genius sitting on top of it reciting verses. His recitations over, he dropped down the ends of nine silk ribbons which were taken by nine masked persons who danced about the tree.[1] This morisco was loudly applauded.

While back at Ferrara –

Duke Ercole, as usual, arranged a nightly performance of classical comedies with intermezzi of music and moriscos. There were moriscos of armed gladiators, of horned shepherds, of Moors with burning tapers in their mouths, of satyrs dancing to the sound of a musical box inside an ass's head, of peasants performing the whole round of their agricultural labour. One morisco was led by a young woman riding upon a car drawn by a unicorn. (Welsford)

A letter tells of a performance of Ariosto's comedy, *I Suppositi*, at Ferrara in 1509:

The intermezzi were all music and song, and at the end of the comedy, Vulcan and the Cyclops struck arrows to the sound of pipes, beating time with hammers and with the bells that they wore on their legs. This display of arrows and bellows was turned into a morisco with the sound of the hammers. (Welsford)

Another letter comments on a performance of a comedy, *Calandra*, at Urbino in 1513:

The intermezzi were as follows: the first was a morisco of Jason who came in dancing dressed as a warrior of antiquity. In a series of rhythmic movements he yoked the fire-breathing bulls, ploughed the ground and sowed the dragon's teeth, which quickly sprang up as armed men who danced a proud morisco. The second intermezzo consisted of the car of

---

[1.] Can this be ancestor to the ribbon-plaiting dance around a maypole that is still performed by schoolchildren?

Venus drawn by doves and accompanied by Cupids who danced a morisco, beating time with their lighted torches. Other cars of Neptune and Juno, other dances of morisco and brandi followed. (Welsford)

These quotations give us a fair idea of what was meant by morisco in Renaissance Italy and we can begin to sympathise with the critics who complained that the intermezzi and the moriscos were so popular that they swamped the drama that was supposed to be the main attraction. There are clearly two shades of meaning involved: at one time morisco is used for a particular type of dance; at another, it indicates a whole scene. We can see a great gulf separating this expensively staged court entertainment from anything we might think of today as morris dancing – and yet the backward-looking element is there: call it 'Renaissance', or call it 'Golden Age Syndrome', the Italian morisco looked back upon fanciful tales of earlier days.

To come back to England: interest in court theatricals grew and expanded through the early years of the sixteenth century, soaking up the influences that were flooding in from Italy. Whatever the subject, whether sacred or secular, interludes in the form of masques were inserted until the masque outgrew the parent and took on a separate life of its own. An interesting example of early masque in this country was found in a document called *The booke of all maner of Orders concernyng an Erles hous*. It tells how a twelfth-night disguising should be presented, and it shows, I think, newly arrived Italian ideas loosely attached to an English disguising that still retains much of its old shape. The quotation is given in full by Collier in his additional notes, but since it is somewhat difficult to follow, and since the content is of greater interest than the form, I give a modern paraphrase.

The disguising is not to come into the hall until the interlude, comedy or tragedy has finished. Three waiters with torches are to light the disguisers as they ride into the hall. The waiters are to bow and depart, or stand aside, while the Lord's four minstrels, who have been waiting in the hall, stand to the side and play. The disguisers are to bow and dance as arranged. If some of the disguisers are women, then they are to enter first, bow and dance; then the men do the same. The disguisers then stand to the side, men on one side and women on the other (or, if they are all men, half on each side). 'Always the men giving to the women the pre-eminence of their standing.' When the disguisers have done, the morris is to burst in, if any be appointed. The minstrels are to play, and as soon as the morris dancers hear their tune they are to come out, one after the other, from the tower or other thing devised for them. They dance, and go back into their tower. When the morris is done, the gentlemen are to bow to the women and each is to take a woman by the hand and dance the basse dances, followed by such rounds as have been arranged by the Master of the Revels. The gentleman is then to take the woman back to her place, bow, and then return to his own place.

Mention of 'comedy or tragedy' signals the arrival of Italian drama, while the end of the piece might be suggesting that gentleman performers danced with ladies of the audience – a sure sign of Italian influence. Whether this 'morris' had English or Italian parents, I would not care to guess. Unfortunately the dating of this manuscript is a little uncertain and even its genuineness has been challenged. Some part was said to be dated 16 Henry VII (1500), although in Collier's opinion the handwriting appeared to be that of the latter end of the reign of Henry VIII.[1] It would certainly fit the theme of this chapter more comfortably if Collier's view was accepted and a date of about 1535 allotted to the book.

As an aside, an interesting comparison can be drawn between England, France and Italy. In England, as we have already seen, Italian Renaissance influences made contact with the mediaeval English disguising, and the result was masque. In France, the same Italian Renaissance influences struck the French entremet (which was close cousin to the English disguising), and the result was ballet. The Renaissance influences that stayed at home in Italy developed and, by the early seventeenth century, had turned into opera. Masque, ballet and opera, therefore, share many common genes.

As the sixteenth century moved on through the reign of Elizabeth, the masque grew in poetry, in scenery and in general dramatic shape. Lawyers at the Inns of Court took up masques as their own special kind of entertainment, and stage architects moved in to create grandiose scenic effects. By this time masques had come to portray an idyllic picture of social harmony and fellowship, reflecting a contentment with the existing order that must have warmed the hearts of those in authority. In order to give point and spice to this impression of tranquillity, a deliberate and carefully measured element of discord or coarse humour was brought in.

'A Particular Entertainment' was given for Queen Anne (consort to James I) at Althorpe, at the Right Honourable the Lord Spencer's, on Saturday 25 June 1603. It was written by Ben Jonson and is sometimes called *The Satyr*. On the Monday following, a character called Nobody, attired in a pair of breeches which were made to come up to his neck, with

---

[1.] The manuscript is now lost and so a more recent opinion cannot be obtained.

his arms out at his pockets, and a cap drowning his face, delivered a speech to introduce a morris of the clowns:

> We are the usher to a morris,
> A kind of masque whereof good store is
> In the country hereabout,
>
> * * * * *
>
> Come on clowns, foresake your dumps,
> And bestir your hobnailed stumps,
>
> * * * * *
>
> But see, the hobby-horse is forgot.
> Fool, it must be your lot
> To supply his want with faces
> And some other buffoon graces,
> You know how; piper, play,
> And let Nobody hence away.

The word 'antic' was often used to describe the discordant parts of a masque, and 'antic dance' and 'morris' were probably regarded as synonyms by authors who were concerned more with overall style, costume and theatrical impact than they were with the steps and figures of a particular dance. 'Antic' is a strange word in this context because it appears to bridge two quite separate meanings. On the one hand it means wild or ill-controlled movement; while on the other hand it links with 'antique' to mean something very old. The *Concise Oxford Dictionary* notes the problem and attempts to explain it, without very much conviction or success, by reporting that someone had attributed grotesque work to the ancients. Following this word 'antic', the wild part of an entertainment came to be called the antic masque or antimasque, and there is no finer example than the witches scene that opens the *Masque of Queenes*, given at Whitehall on 2 February 1609. It makes no mention of the word *morris*, but the "magical Daunce full of preposterous change and gesticulation" is, I suspect, morris in everything but name, given the usage of Jacobean court entertainment. It will give the reader a useful impression of masque in its fully developed form, and it will give the writer pleasure in describing a very fine work, to round off this chapter on drama with an account of Ben Jonson's *Masque of Queenes*.

Twelve witches, each personating one of the nastier components of human behaviour, Suspicion, Malice, Execration, Rage, and so on, met at the mouth of a Hell to recite charms and call up their Dame. The Dame arrived with "her hayre knotted, and folded with vipers; in her hand a torch made of a dead man's arme", and boasted of the witches' power to confuse Nature.

Dame Earth shall quake,
And the houses shake,
And her belly shall ake,
As her back were brake,
Such a birth to make.

Shouts and clamours led to a strange and sudden music, whereupon the witches fell into a magical dance full of preposterous change and gesticulation. After the dance, there was more loud and sudden music when "The Hagges themselves and the Hell into which they ran, quite vanished; and the whole face of the scene altered, scarce suffering the memory of any such thing." Now presented was a glorious and magnificent building figuring the House of Fame; on top, twelve masquers sat upon a throne triumphal, erected in form of a pyramid and circled with all store of light. Then entered Perseus, representing heroic and masculine virtue, who introduced the masquers, noble ladies dressed as the choice of woman-kind, eleven great Queens of time long gone. Stage machinery changed the throne and Fame appeared, to speak in praise of each Queen, ending with Bel-anna, Royal Queen of the Ocean, played by Queen Anne herself. The masquers descended and mounted, four into each of three chariots, drawn by eagles, griffons and lions, with each chariot accompanied by torchbearers and four bound hags. They all rode in state about the stage singing a song and then alighted to dance two curious dances, after which they took out the men and danced the measures. Mr Allin sang a ditty, followed by a third dance, ending with galliardes and corrantos. Finally they took to the chariots again and went "triumphing about the stage".

CHAPTER 6

SO WHAT ACTUALLY HAPPENED?
A list of morris events

Having equipped ourselves with some general knowledge about a lot of activities and opinions which had, or might have had, a bearing on early morris, it now seems the right time to take up a new direction: to start looking through the card index of recorded morris events, beginning at the beginning, examining each occasion in the light of its own time and seeing what emerges. Although this way of laying out the evidence is pleasantly simple, it is not entirely without problems because some cards in the index cry out to be treated as a group and will not give of their best when interleaved with events of an unrelated kind. As an attempt to strike a reasonable compromise, I am going to extract from the main chronological sequence all the interesting detail for two different groups of source material; the material from these groups will then be presented as Chapters 7 and 8, where I hope their isolation will help clarity.

Chapter 7: Account Book Entries from English Parish Churches.

Chapter 8: Some Illustrations of Morisco.

When this book was first planned, many years ago, one intention was to present a brief account of each and every morris event for which there was a record. At that time there were probably less than a hundred such events to deal with. Now, the 1990s have seen a tremendous expansion of research into early morris and the figure has grown to a thousand or more and so we are on to Plan B.

The new intention is to be a bit selective and take those Items that have a tale to tell, to present them in date order and hope that they will paint their own picture. Anyone wishing to consult a comprehensive list for the period 1458–1748 (where the entries are codified for computer analysis and fully referenced) should find *Annals of Early Morris*, Michael Heaney and John Forrest, published by the Centre for English Cultural Tradition and Language, University of Sheffield, 1991.

Other important works from the 1990s are *Morris Dancing in the English South Midlands, 1660–1900: A Chronological Gazetteer* by Keith Chandler, 1993; its companion volume *Ribbons, Bells and Squeaking Fiddles*, also 1993; and *The History of Morris Dancing 1458-1750* by John Forrest, 1999.

Much of the work that has been done on folk material in the 1980s and 1990s leaves me with rather mixed feelings. It is obviously important that material from original sources should be correctly reported and given references so that it can be found again. It is also valuable that the material is gathered together and published so that others can have access. But our folk traditions seem to have slipped into an academic world and joined company with sociopolitical process and the obscurer branches of statistics. One might expect astrophysics to be discussed in barely intelligible language in university coffee rooms, but is this really a useful way to treat our folk customs? A random quote from a recent book has: "The second model, typified by evolutionary biology, does not treat origin as essence, or as a static fact at all, but as a small component in a diachronic process, which is nonteleological." Out of context, I know, but I rest my case!

* * * * *

Main chronological sequence

1137

The year 1137 saw a political union established between Catalonia and Aragon, secured by the betrothal of Aragon's Queen Petronila to Ramon Berenguer, Count of Barcelona. A grand celebration to mark the occasion was held at Lérida in north-east Spain and a description appears in a Spanish book published in 1855.[1] As part of his description the author quotes from a manuscript source:

> The Prince and Queen went to church accompanied by most of the prelates and nobility of Catalonia and Aragon, preceded by a large group of jugglers and singers as well as many dancers. Particular mention was made of a group of Moors and Christians who enacted a battle: a dance that is preserved to this day by some of the Spanish people.

Taken at face value, this is a clear reference to a Moor/Christian display/battle/dance of the sort that is later described as a morisco or moresque, and which does indeed survive to the present day among the folk customs of southern Europe. If we can provisionally accept that some sort of link once existed between English morris and the Spanish morisco, then this date of 1137 marks the very earliest event which can claim connection with modern morris dancing.

Unfortunately, an element of doubt already hangs in the air – for one thing, correspondence with Spain has so far failed to locate the manuscript used by Fuertes and so there is no way of judging its date and reliability. For

---

[1.] *Historia de la Música Española*, by Mariano Soriano Fuertes, Tome I, pp. 125–6.

another, the gap of 252 years between 1137 and the next battle/display on my list is much too long to be comfortable. Thirdly, I have a suspicion that the author of this manuscript, whoever he was, belonged to that group of writers who attribute an easy timelessness to folk customs. If the customs are seen as timeless, then it is only slightly dishonest when an historian slips an interesting custom into an early historical record with the intention of filling out the account and adding local colour. We have already seen something of the sort when Holinshed (1577) added 'dancing about maypoles' to a 1306 event. The 'timeless' theory of folk customs has always had a strong emotional appeal and we need to be on our guard against any anachronism it has left lying in our path.

The evidence of an unseen manuscript cannot properly be assessed, but the omens are not good and I, for one, feel quite confident that the account is spurious and that no Moor/Christian battle was presented for entertainment anything like as early as 1137.

1240   Summer Game – see page 70

1306   Summer Game – see page 84

1334   Mumming – see page 83

1341

In 1341 Petrarch was called to Rome to receive the Crown of Poetry. According to the notes at the back of a French biography published in 1764,[1] somebody had claimed that he rounded off the occasion in a ridiculous way quite foreign to his usual character. The story goes that after the formality of the coronation he stripped off his clothes down to the doublet, attached some little bells to his arms and legs, and danced a fine and vigorous morisco to amuse the ladies.

The French text is not easy to follow in detail, but there is little doubt that we are looking at a case of fraud. Starting somewhere around 1549 a shady tale unfolds of imposters, of faked letters and of somebody who made a lot of money rather quickly. It is fairly clear, therefore, that Petrarch's morisco is no more than an incidental by-product arising out of a sixteenth-century fiction. Remembering the rule for fiction, that the event described should be related to the time of writing and not to the date claimed by the author, then we can begin to see some validity in this description of morisco, provided we set it in 1549 and not in 1341. Another anachronism!

[1.] *Mémoires Pour la Vie de François Pétrarque*, Tome II, Notes, p. 3 and p. 9, by de Sade (no, not the Marquis).

1343   Tournament – see page 78

1344

Strutt's popular book, *Sports and Pastimes*, made use of some illustrations copied from a manuscript in the Bodleian Library. One of these pictures shows us five people who hold hands and dance vigorously (if somewhat untidily) to the music of bagpipe and portative organ. Strutt believed that this scene represented a fool's dance of the sort which had once formed part of the Feast of Fools and he went on, "I make no doubt, the morris-dance, which afterwards became exceedingly popular in this country, originated from the fool's dance". The capes with grotesquely extended hoods, and what are presumably bells on the extremities, do much to support Strutt's view that these are, indeed, fools, and I see no reason to challenge his belief that this dance was a forerunner of the morris. My only difference with Strutt is that he saw morris as springing from this one single source, whereas I would prefer to hold the door open in case there are any other forerunners about.

The manuscript that provided Strutt with his illustration is a magnificently illuminated book called *The Romance of Alexander*, which contains a collection of tales quite irrelevant to our present study. However, in mediaeval days decoration seems to have followed the whim of the craftsman and was not necessarily tied to the theme of the text and so, in the Alexander Romance, we find on each page a lower border decorated with figures engaged in some activity. In a large number of cases this activity is a game or a dance, and these are the scenes that caught Strutt's eye. A clear guide to the geographical home of these dancing figures is given, because the text of the book is in the French dialect of Flanders, the illumination is in a style considered to be Anglo-Norman and there is reason to believe that the book was put together in Bruges. The date is even more clearly defined because it is recorded that the illuminator completed his task on 18 April 1344   a pleasing touch of precision when compared with the extreme vagueness of date we will encounter for some other illustrations.

Joseph Strutt, and more recently Cecil Sharp, have made these five dancing figures and their musicians fairly well known. What is less well known is that there are three more pages in the Alexander Romance which also carry very similar scenes – five dancers in each case, holding hands or linked by short cords – each set of five wearing a distinctive style of hood. Although we cannot now be certain about the purpose of this dance, four illustrations in the same book is a strong hint that it was a widespread and popular activity in its day.

1389

Jehan Froissart (1338–1410) was an honest chronicler: a man who moved around Europe keeping his eyes open and seeking out the people who could tell him about recent events: a man who saw no need to expand the record with comment and criticism. He was there, in 1389, when Queen Isabella of France made a ceremonial entry into Paris, and I have already quoted from Enid Welsford's condensed version of his account in the 'Civic Processions' part of Chapter 5 (see page 75). Let us now take a closer look at the Christian/Saracen battle by using the fuller version put into English by Bourchier and published by Pynson in 1523.

.... In the street there was a stage and thereupon a castle. And along on the stage there was ordained the Pass of King Salhadyn and all their deeds in personages the Christian men on the one part and the Sarazins on the other part. And there was in personage all the lords of name that of old time had been armed and had done any feats of arms at the Pass of Salhadyn and were armed with such armour as they then used. And then a little above them there was in personages the French King and the twelve Peers of France armed with the blazon of their arms. And when the French Queen's litter was come before this stage she rested there a season. Then the personages on the stage of King Richard departed from his company and went to the French King and demanded licence to go and assail the Sarazins and the King gave him leave. Then King Richard returned to his twelve companions. Then they all set them in order and incontinent went and assailed the King Salhadyn and the Sarazins. There in sport there seemed a great battle and it endured a good space. This pageant was well regarded.

This, then, is a clear and reliable description of a combat between Christians and Infidels, put on as a stage show to impress the French Queen and her attendants. It would also be easy to see this performance, were it expanded into a larger space, as a typical tournament that had been based on real events in the Third Crusade when Richard I of England and Philip II of France fought their way towards Jerusalem in 1191. No mention is made of morisco, or dance of any kind. However, there is enough similarity between this event and the later ones where dancing was included, and where the word *morisco* or *moresque* was used, for us to suggest Paris, 1389, as an early step on the way to a morisco performance.

1391   King of Fools – see page 74

1392

Another story from Froissart (Pynson edition) tells that about midnight in Paris on the Tuesday before Candlemas 1392 a marriage was being celebrated between two members of the French King's household. By way of pastime a squire had devised a mummery and prepared "six coats made of linen cloth covered with pitch and thereon flax like hair". These coats were sewn onto the King and five of his nobles so that "they seemed like wild wodehouses,[1] full of hair from the top of the head to the sole of the foot". The danger of fire was realised and orders were given for torches to be kept well away, but unfortunately the Duke of Orleans arrived late and missed the warning. The six entered the hall led by the King, who was separate (the other five being fastened one to another): the disguise was so complete that not one man knew them. The King moved away from his companions and "went to the ladies to sport with them as youth required" and a duchess took hold of his arm saying she would not release him until she knew his name.

The Duke of Orleans was so curious to know the identity of the five that danced that "he put one of the torches so near that the heat of the fire entered into the flax (wherein if fire take there is no remedy) and suddenly was on a bright flame and so each of them set fire one to the other. The pitch was so fastened to the linen cloth and their shirts so dry and fine and so joining to their flesh that they began to burn and to cry for help". One ran to the scullery and cast himself into the water where they rinsed the pots and so survived, but two died on the spot and another two died a couple of days later after great misery and pain.

What reasons do we have for associating this sad happening with morris? One reason is the similarity with the entertainments and antimasques of the sixteenth and early seventeenth centuries where performances very like that of these wodehouses went under the name of 'antic morris'. Froissart was not the only chronicler to record this event, and a second account, by a monk of St Denis, says that they danced to the accompaniment of 'choreas saracenicas' (which might reasonably be translated as 'moorish dances'), although this sounds more like a reference to the music than it does to the dance. The word *morisco* is not used: Bourchier's translation describes the

---

[1.] Woodhouse or woodwose: a wild man of the woods; a theatrical savage.

event as a 'mummery' and this was, no doubt, the most appropriate word in England during the early 1500s when the translation was made, but Froissart's actual word was 'ébattement', best understood as a frolic. Forty-eight years earlier, back in 1344, we saw sets of five people in funny clothes holding hands and dancing vigorously, and this present scene has obvious similarities – similarities that seem strong enough to overrule mere coincidence – but interpretation is difficult. The hairy costume is reminiscent of the tatters recorded in the morris tradition of the Welsh borders and taken up by numerous modern sides, but this is probably no more than two unconnected attempts to make an outrageous garment out of commonly available materials.

What, then, can we conclude from these miscellaneous observations? Froissart's reputation gives us confidence in the authenticity, but we have to acknowledge that the wodehouses of 1392 gave a very different sort of performance from the Christian/Saracen combat of 1389. Which was the true ancestor of morris? I can only offer the thought that they may both have provided materials for the building. Let us close this section with a sympathetic thought for Charles VI, King of France, who watched his companions burn on this sad occasion; who went on to suffer attacks of madness and who then lost a large part of his kingdom at the battle of Agincourt.

1418   Mumming – see page 83

Circa 1427

John Lydgate was a Benedictine monk and a prolific writer described by some as a not unworthy successor to Chaucer. He seems to have drawn together the old ideas of mumming and disguising, then introduced elements of allegory and, most importantly, developed the idea of plot. He devised an entertainment to be presented before King Henry VI on New Year's Eve at Hertford Castle. The bare bones of this 'Mumming at Hertford' go like this:

Six men protest to the King that their wives are shrews and beg the King to restore to them the right of mastery in their own homes. A representative of the six wives challenges the idea that mastery belongs to men as of right. A spokesman for the King acknowledges the importance of the question and the need to avoid snap decisions. Judgement is thus postponed for a year and single men are warned to weigh up the likely price of getting married.

The use of the word *mumming* in the title has caused several writers to wonder whether the actors spoke. John Forrest has suggested a style of performance where a 'poet' stands at a pulpit, reciting a verse narrative, while actors in masks proceed from a stage house and perform the actions thus specified. On a lighter theme one might wonder what the King made of this bleak view of matrimony, bearing in mind that he had only just passed his sixth birthday.

1432 Entry into London – see page 76

1438

When Barbara Lowe was preparing her 1957 paper, she examined the collection of prints in the Warburg Institute (part of London University) and found a number of illustrations that she thought might have relevance to early morris. These pictures make a fascinating study but they are very difficult to evaluate because of a shortage of accompanying information. Most of them are without contemporary title, so we cannot be sure what the original artist intended to portray: the date is often no closer than a guess at a century, based on an art historian's feelings about the style, and even the country of origin is sometimes in doubt. Some attempt will be made later on, in Chapter 8, to fit these illustrations into some sort of order, but for the moment, let us look at one of them that stands apart from the rest because it has a known source with a date that is both early and secure. This particular print is a copy taken from a manuscript preserved in Poland.

Manuscript IV F 21 in the University Library, Wroclaw, was made in Padua by Johannes de Metis and Johannes de Bu, canons of St Salvator Metensis, in 1438.[1] It contains the *Opera Astrologica* of Michael Scotus, including the *Liber Particularis*. On folio 146 V there is a decoration across the head of the page consisting of eight figures in a line – a lady and a musician are easily identifiable; there are four dancers with bell-pads worn below the knee in a manner very like modern Cotswold morris; there are a crouching figure that Mrs Lowe thought was a fool dressed as a baboon (well, I suppose it could be) and an eighth figure who might be just another dancer, but is rather more generously provided with ribbons. Distinctively pointed hats are worn and very long wavers held in the hands.

We have already met two distinct kinds of what we might call 'proto-morris', the Moor/Christian battle, and the fool's dance of five in line. Here in 1438 we meet up with the earliest evidence for a third kind of proto-morris: a form of dance that Mrs Lowe labelled 'Ring Morris'. Ring morris is well represented among the early illustrations, and a general survey leads to the following list of common features, which can serve us as a definition.

---

[1] I am grateful to Dr Stefan Kubów, Director of the Library, for information about this manuscript.

1) A small group of loose-limbed young men, usually wearing bells, dance with great vigour around
2) A lady who holds up an apple or ring (presumably as a token prize); also
3) A musician playing upon pipe and tabor and
4) A jester or fool with a bauble.

The 'ring' of ring morris refers to the token held by the lady, not to any circular form of the dance, although it is obvious that any dance round a lady will tend to take up a circular shape.

Without wishing to make too much of the pun, I feel there is a worrying hint of circularity in this matter of ring morris. Let me put it this way. George Tollet was the first to draw public attention to the figures in the Betley window, and the title of his essay makes it quite clear that he believed them to be morris dancers. A few years later Francis Douce introduced the van Meckenem rectangular engraving and, because of the close similarity with Betley, these figures too were thought to represent morris. Both Betley and the rectangular engraving show us a set of performers in isolation – rather like toy soldiers that are still in their box – leaving us to decide how they ought to be arranged. However, a strong hint about the preferred arrangement is provided by a second van Meckenem engraving, this time an engraving designed to fill a circular space and showing dancers in a circle. Barbara Lowe took the idea of young men in grotesque posture circling around a lady in company with a fool and a musician, and assembled a number of illustrations that followed this theme. The fact that a dozen or so illustrations survive of this fairly unusual scene is some sort of evidence that a real performance must lie at their origin, although we need to acknowledge that many of the illustrations carry a strong air of fantasy about them. A rather more direct point of uncertainty concerns the question of whether this performance was ever considered to be morris, morisco, or any other variant on the name, before the time of Tollet. The circularity closes when we go on to state that fifteenth-century morris was a wild dance of young men about a woman, because that's what the illustrations show.

Having declared my own uncertainty on this matter I shall now revert to the orthodox view and accept ring morris as a possible phase in our story: a phase that has already been labelled proto-morris.

1440

Gilles de Rais was a mediaeval baron of quite extraordinary character – even by the standards of his own day. He acquired lordship over extensive lands in north-west France and, at times of financial pressure, sold off estates at unaccountably low prices, to the annoyance of his relations. He fought at the side of Joan of Arc, spent great sums in the King's service, and was made Marshal of France. He maintained a court of almost royal proportions and spent yet more money on charitable works, on funding the spectacular celebration of Church rites, and (in the manner of an each-way bet) on the support of necromancers. A splendidly generous patron of literature and music, he studied alchemy and was a skilled illuminator and bookbinder – he was also a mass-murderer. He was hanged on 26 October 1440 for a variety of crimes including the kidnap, torture and murder of a hundred and forty children.

A history of Brittany by Dom Gui Alexis Lobineau published in Paris, 1707, includes a very minor item among the excesses of this strange man:

> Item, there were games, farces, Morisques, the acting out of mystery plays for Pentecost and for the Ascension upon high scaffolds under which were hippocras and other strong wines, as in a wine cellar. (Vol II, Col 1069)

If we accept that Lobineau's source actually used the word *morisques*, and this is not unreasonable, we can go on to guess what sort of performance this might have been. The evidence, such as it is, offers three possibilities: fool's dance, Moor/Christian combat, and ring morris. The fool's dance was, perhaps, too simple to warrant separate mention in an account book, while a set-piece battle might be expected to show more than a one-word mention. Pushed to make a selection, I would therefore opt for ring morris.

1454   Entremet – see page 73

1457   Rogationtide procession – see page 86

1457
A little further on in Lobineau's history of Brittany there is an "Extract from the Account of Olivier le Roux, Treasurer and Receiver General under the Duke Arthur III".

> To certain fellows who have made several 'esbatemens de morisques' and other games before the Duke at Tours – 6 escus
> (Vol II, Col 1205.)

The inherent reliability of account books gives us confidence that the word *morisques* was generally understood in the Brittany of 1457, and the context makes it clear that morisques provided light-hearted entertainment in an aristocratic setting. 'Esbatemens' reminds us of Froissart's use of 'ébattement' some sixty-five years earlier. It would probably be squeezing the evidence too hard to suggest that 'ébattement' was a fool's dance which developed into an 'esbatemens de morisques' or ring morris, but it is an interesting thought.

1458

The 'Knight of the Swan' is a long-lived story, one version of which is Wagner's *Lohengrin*. Barbara Lowe found a translation of the tale from Norman French into English, about the year 1458, in which morris was mentioned. I have not succeeded in getting back quite that far, but I have seen a facsimile of a translation by Robert Copland published by Wynkin de Worde in 1512 which has the same text as that quoted by Mrs Lowe. Modernising the spelling, it reads:

> For the night before the day of wedding, for the honour and magnificence of the good King Oryant and of his noble love Beatryce, were made moryskes, comedies, dances, interludes, and all manner of joyous sports in the king's palace where as were many great princes and knights of renown.

It must be stressed that this is a work of fiction, but it is obvious that the translator expected 'moryskes' to spark a picture in the minds of his readers. There is a very strong similarity between this reference and the two we have already seen from Lobineau and it is also worth a reminder that English forces had only recently pulled out of northern France (1453). As a working hypothesis, let us suppose that what we have called ring morris grew up to become a favourite item of entertainment in the richer Anglo-Gallic houses, around the middle of the fifteenth century.

1458

This is the date that every morris dancer ought to carry in his back pocket so that he can lightly toss it to an audience when somebody asks, 'But how old is morris?' It is the date of the oldest mention we have to 'morris dance' in England.

The date refers to the will of Alice Wetenhale, a widow of Bury St Edmunds, who also had a house in Sythe Lane, London: so a lady, we may assume, of substantial means. A section of her will, put into English, reads:

.... Further, I leave to Katherine my daughter my best gilded cup with a lid of matching pattern, 1 short-stemmed gilded cup with lid, *3 cups of silver engraved with morris dancers with a single lid for them*, one gilded goblet .... (Translation by Robin du Boulay, 2002.)

No further information is given and we are left to suppose that the cups probably depicted a scene of ring morris. However, there is one thing that we can say with some assurance: Mrs Wetenhale was confident that anyone reading her will would recognise a morris dance when they saw it; otherwise she would not have used these words to identify her property. From this we may go on to deduce that morris dances (or at least, illustrations of morris dances) had been around for a few years and were generally known among the merchant class – the social level Mrs Wetenhale seems to have occupied.

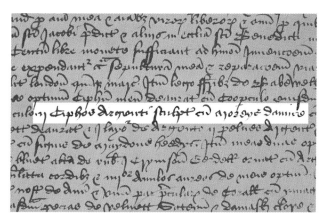

iij ciphos argenti sculptos cum moreys dauncie

1458

By strange coincidence a second will from the very same year also has a piece of silver "with a Moresk theron" (Will of Sir Thomas Chaworth in the York Registry, see *Annals of Early Morris*).

1459

A French book was published in 1620 which reviewed the history of various orders of chivalry.[1] In a chapter which deals with the Order of the Starre, a story is told of the elevation of Gaston of Navarre to the peerage as the Count of Foix, and how he went on to get engaged to the King's

---

[1.] *The Theater of Honour and Knight-hood* by André Favyn: an English translation was published in 1623.

youngest daughter and to be made a Knight of the Starre. In celebration of his knighthood, Gaston entertained the King and court to a great feast held at Tours. (The date mentioned by Favyn for the elevation is 1458, but by the time of the feast, events had moved on into the following year.) This feast is described in luxuriant detail: the first service, the second service and the third; then an entremet of a castle; a fourth service and an entremet of a tiger; a fifth service and a third entremet. The banquet goes on to notch up seven services and five entremets, but it is the third entremet that concerns us here. Twenty-four men carried in a mountain, which included two fountains, one of rosewater and one of musk; young rabbits and small birds issued forth

> And in hollow places of the said hill stood four young lads and a damsel, attired like savages, who came forth at a passage in the rock, dancing (by good direction) a Morisque before the assembly.

We know nothing of Favyn's sources, but matters of aristocratic promotion are usually handled with care by the chroniclers and I think we may depend upon this one. The mountain is typical of the entremets presented between courses of a mediaeval banquet, and the cast of 'four young lads and a damsel' fits in very nicely with our present hypothesis that anything called morris at this date was likely to be ring morris. We are, of course, still centred in northern France, and the fact that they were 'attired like savages' is a reminder of the wodehouses in Paris, two generations before.

1459

A letter on the files of the Vaughan Williams Memorial Library[1] draws attention to a Norman French work of fiction, *Le petit Jehun de Saintré*, by the Burgundian writer Antoine de La Sale. The book bears a dedication to the Duc d'Anjou dated 25 September 1459 (although the manuscript had been finished and signed some four years earlier). Two quotations are given by Mr Moseley which, put into English, read:

> After rising from table they went into the Great Hall, the King on one side and the Queen on the other, to see the different kinds of dancing and the morisques.

And again, some pages later:

---

[1] From Mr Laurence Moseley of Oxford, dated 25 September 1960.

The strolling minstrels began to play for dancing. There followed basse dances, songs, elaborate morisques and other amusements. Nobody remembers a day when there had been a more delightful and joyous celebration, nor one so well organised.

De La Sale brings his book to a close with the death of Saintré in 1368, thus setting the occasion which had 'morisques' to some time earlier than this date. If this were true, then it would become one of our oldest references; but it is another anachronism, and the scene that de La Sale describes must be of his own day, set back into the previous century to suit the plot. One reason for saying this is because there is already a pattern emerging from the evidence that places the morisque in the courts of northern France around the middle of the fifteenth century. This may be something of a shock to those who are devoted to the Englishness of morris, but it is not an original idea. In 1807 Douce wrote, "It is much more probable that we had it [morris dance] from our Gallic neighbours, or even from the Flemings".

1466

The very first record of preparations being made for a morris dance in England is found from a very unlikely location: Lanherne in North Cornwall, not far from Newquay. Domestic accounts of the Arundell family for the Christmas period 1466/7 show the purchase of materials for a disguising and for a 'Moruske'. The items that were specifically for the moruske were:

4 dozen bells	3s.
2 quires paper	7d.
Half a pound glue	2d.

1467

Charles the Bold of Burgundy owned two salt cellars decorated round the covers with "une danse de morisque". So notes Violet Alford, from a court inventory.

1468   Entremet, Tournament – see pages 73 and 78

1469   Summer Game – see page 84

1473

At a carnival banquet given in Rome by a nephew of the Pope, the meal ended with a 'worthy morisco', which seems to have involved a dispute between Turks and Christians. Later on, a triumphal chariot was displayed in the courtyard and out of it came morris dancers, one by one. On the following day the 'Turk' and the 'King of Macedonia' appeared in two chariots, and their followers engaged in a mock battle (Welsford, *The Court Masque*).

Here then we can see, presented on a single occasion, two of the principal ingredients that (presumably) lie behind early morris: the Turk/Christian combat, and the Fool's Dance that comes on in single file.

1477

The Drapers' Guild paid for a morris as part of its contribution to the Midsummer Watch procession in London:

> Payment of the costs incurred on St Peter's night for the Watch waiting upon the Mayor. First, paid for the morisse dance and for the costs of the 9 Worthies ——. (Based on Forrest, 1999.)

This is the first clearly defined performance of morris in England, 27 June 1477, in London.

1491   Italian theatricals – see page 87

1494

Henry VII's court at Westminster:
    "For playing of the mourice dance 40s."

Circa 1500

In a book *The Royal Danish Ballet* by Svend Kragh Jacobsen, 1955, there is the following passage:

> The ballet in Denmark has its roots far back in the past. Its earliest signs were found in the school comedies performed by the pupils of the grammar schools on special occasions. The famous Danish poet, Morten Børup, composed a 'Morien Dance of Fools' about the year 1500 which, three quarters of a century later, still caused a sensation when it was performed within the courtyard of the Royal Castle on the occasion of the christening of Christian IV in 1577.
> (This quotation passed to me by Ian Woodward.)

This sounds very like the Renaissance Italian intermezzi, but performance by grammar school pupils is a unique element.

1501   Court disguising – see page 79

1501

Henry VII's court in London:

"To them that danced the mores dance   26s 8d."

(Sums of money were commonly spoken in terms of 'marks' worth 13 shillings and 4 pence.)

At Westminster instructions were given:

"That Jacques Hault and William Pawne devise and prepare disguisings and some morisks after the best manner they can."

1502

Henry VII's court at Richmond upon Thames:

"To one Lewes for a mores dance   53s 4d." (4 marks)

1502   Italian theatricals – see page 88

1502

Scottish court of James IV at Stirling:

"To the men that brought in the morice dance, and to their minstrels, in Sterling   42s."

This was presumably payment in English money since the Scottish system at that time did not use the shilling.

1504

Scottish court:

"To master John, to buy belts for the moris dance   28s."

"To Colin Campbell and his mates that brought in the moris dance, for their expence made thereon   14 pounds."

This dramatic increase in the amount may mark a change from accounting in English money to using Scottish. Exchange rates varied, of course, but it was not unusual for English money to be worth up to twelve times the Scottish equivalent.

The dancers in master John's dance, as well as having belts, had clothes made for them: 6 dancing coats of red and blue taffeta: a woman's gown of blue taffeta with white lining, and blue, red and variant taffeta for the dancers' headgear.

These Scottish accounts of the Lord High Treasurer, transcribed by Anna Jean Mill (1927), contain a grand collection of materials, and glimpses of performance at the court entertainments in the first few years of the sixteenth century. These are gysaris (disguisers) who played a play or danced; we meet Robin Hood of Perth; there is payment to a barber who healed Paul's head when he was hurt by the Abbot of Unreason; there is payment to a Queen of May on the gate as the King passed by; there are lots of clothes – five coats, doublets and hose plus a kirtle for a woman for dancing; bells and legharness for dancers; there is a mumming gown to the King; we find goat skins for the wildmen and, although it is a late item and irrelevant, I cannot resist

"To the Egyptians that danced before the King in Holyrood House 40s."

Circa 1505

"Sum singis; sum dancis; sum tellis storeis;
Sum lait at evin bringis in the moreis."
So wrote William Dunbar, the Scottish poet.

1507

An item in the accounts of the London Carpenters' Company:
"Paid to the morys dancers 8d."

1507

This date marks the beginning of a sequence of references to morris in the churchwardens' accounts from Kingston-upon-Thames. Some text from these references will be found in Chapter 7.

This set of churchwardens' accounts survive from 1504 to 1539 and display an involvement with games, ales and feasts at such a level that one wonders whether there was once an ambitious pageant-master who persuaded the Rector to appoint him as churchwarden! Such is the wealth of interesting detail to be found in these extensive accounts that they have been re-cycled by many writers with varying degrees of accuracy and with differing objectives. They form a particularly happy hunting ground for those who wish to explore the relationships between Robin Hood, Maid Marian and the morris dancers. A few of these ideas are aired in Chapter 7.

1509 Italian theatricals – see page 88

1510

Another will. Richard Jackson:
"My cup with the morris dance."

1510

In Hall's Chronicle (1548 republished 1809) in the first year of King Henry VIII, there are long descriptions of grand court events with heavy emphasis on fashion. Two items are of passing interest:

"The torchbearers were apparelled in crimson satin and green, like Moreskoes, their faces black."

Further on, six ladies enter,

"their faces, necks, arms and hands, covered with fine pleasaunce black: some call it 'Lumberdynes', which is marvellous thin, so that the same ladies seemed to be 'nygrost or blacke Mores'."

1511

Hall's Chronicle for the second year of Henry VIII:

Against the 12 day or the day of the Epiphany at night, before the banquet in the hall at Richmond, was a pageant devised like a mountain, glistering by night, as though it had been all of gold and set with stones, on the top of the which mountain was a tree of gold, the branches and boughs frysed with gold, spreading on every side over the mountain, with roses and pomegranates, the which mountain was with devices brought up towards the King, and out of the same came a lady apparelled in cloth of gold, and the children of honor called the Henchemen, which were freshly disguised, and danced a morice before the King. And that done, re-entered the mountain and then it was drawn back, and then was the wassail or banquet brought in, and so broke up Christmas.

1512

Scottish court:

"Paid to monsieur Lamote's servant that danced a moris to the King   9 pounds."
"The 16th day of December, to monsieur Lamote's servant that danced another moris to the King and Queen   5 pounds 8s."

This sounds very similar to Arbeau's account that I have dated to 1540 (see page 15).

1513   Italian theatricals – see page 88

1514

Henry VIII's court at Richmond-upon-Thames:

The Christmas revels had an interlude which contained "A moresks of 6 persons and 2 ladies". The ladies were called Beauty and Venus. Coats were made for the performers including 3 minstrels and a fool. 348 bells are mentioned for the morris and 6 pairs of slop hose for covering of their bells. Six jackets for gentlemen [presumably the dancers] were made, to every jacket 6 yards. These jackets had wide sleeves pendant. [This ties in nicely with the illustrations.] There were 6 gowns of black sarsenet to cover their garments. Also bought were 42 thousand spangles! (Collier)

Comparing 1511 with 1514, the performances show significant differences, notwithstanding that both were called morris (within the latitude of Tudor spelling). The Henchemen look like straightforward performers, but in the latter case the morris is danced by 'persons', by 'gentlemen', who are provided with slop hose to cover their bells and a black gown to cover everything else. I think what we are seeing here is an early appearance of masque, as mentioned above on page 87.

1517

Rodney Gallop reports that a Corpus Christi procession in Coimbra, Portugal, had a Mourisca provided by the Shoemakers' Guild and a sword dance provided by the Potters'.

Is this a trading of ideas between London and Portugal? Well, possibly. Was a Mourisca anything like a morris dance or are we being led along by some similarity in the names? Gallop's descriptions of moriscas would cause most morris dancers to throw up their hands in horror and cry, 'Nothing to do with us!' – but that is twentieth-century evidence. What was the position four hundred years earlier?

1521

In the Midsummer Watch Processions in London, a 'King of the Moors' had followers:

> "For wages to 60 moryans great and small with servants
> and all and a woman morian 4d apiece for both nights
> and the woman morian 8d for both nights   20s 4d." (sic)
> "For the loan of 60 darts to Godfrey for the said moryans
> 2s and for the loss of 3 darts 12d   3s."
> "For fire for the moryans after they had put off
> their clothes and were naked   6d."

John Forrest envisages these moryans with fireworks in their hands and clad in skin-tight black leather – well, each to his own taste. I reckon that after their nude performance they would need an ordinary fire to warm up.

An Italian eyewitness to this same event saw "naked boys dyed black like devils, with dart and target in their hands". This scene, with the King of the Moors attended by a large number of black moryans carrying darts and targets, has led Forrest to claim a direct link with other European guild processions and a probable descent from the Moor/Christian battle. I think he is probably right. On the other hand, would someone watching this procession four hundred and eighty years ago, seeing the King of the Moors with his turban of white feathers and his troop of black moryans, say to his neighbour, 'Hey, we usually call them morris dancers!'? No, I don't think so.

1522

Christmas revels at Richmond-upon-Thames for Princess Mary (age six and not yet labelled 'Bloody'). Her Lord of Misrule arranged disguisings and the materials included "ten dozen bells with nine morris coats". (Lowe)

1525

> "To Walter Fount and his company, that is to say 8 persons
> with their minstrel, for a moris-dance both nights for the
> Mayor, all going on foot before the constables.   15s."

These London Midsummer Watch processions happened twice, on the eves of 23 June and of 28 June.

Unlike the moryans of 1521, who were paid individually, this morris dance seems to have been booked as a package, complete with a minstrel. This suggests, of course, that the morris dance had some continuity of existence outside the guild processions.

1526

Dorothy Gardiner, in her *Story of Sandwich*, tells of a day when a gang of twenty armed men were at the fair threatening to kill. The account goes on, "The same night the rioters danced a morrice about the town, with swords and bucklers." Forrest uses this as another piece of evidence to link morris with a warlike combat theme. (In 1984 John Forrest published a book, *Morris and Matachin*, showing his interest in this particular link.)

This Sandwich night sounds more like real aggression to me. How far such an event should be linked to an entertainment of pantomime sword play, and then on to a morris dance, is something I still feel very cautious about. There may be threads of connection, there may be threads running parallel, but too much emphasis can be very misleading.

1532

An inventory records that Henry VIII owned "A gold salt, called the Moresdaunce, with 5 Moresdauncers and a tabrett." A 'lady' is mentioned in a later description.

Circa 1535   Disguising – see pages 89 and 90

Circa 1540   Arbeau's small boy – see page 15

1541

Costs were rising and the London Drapers' Guild were considering whether they could continue to support the Midsummer Watch processions.

> .... that they for every groat in time past are now fain to give 5 and that in divers things as shall appear in the hireing of drums, minstrels, flag draggers, two hand sword players, morysdaunsers and bearers of the giant which hath risen by a wanton and superfluous precedence ....

1552

The Diary of Henry Machyn tells that on 4 January the King's Lord of Misrule, with a great number of young knights and gentlemen, came from Greenwich, landed at Tower Wharf and went on to Cheapside. Among this great company, each wearing a yellow and green baldric, there was a "mores dance dancing with a tabret".

On 26 May of this same year, in Fenchurch parish, there was a goodly maypole painted white and green and the people wore white and green baldrics. There was a giant and the mores-dance. Regrettably, that same day, the Lord Mayor caused the pole to be taken down and broken.

1553

4 January: the King's Lord of Misrule came out again – much the same as last year, but the baldrics this time were blue and white. Items in the procession shed a curious light on public attitudes in this time of Edward VI.

> Trumpeters, tabors, drums, flutes and fools and the mores daunce, guns, mores-pykes, bagpipes and the jailers with pillory, stocks, axe, gyves and bolts, some fast by the legs and some by the necks, and so rode through Mark Lane, Gracechurch Street and Cornhill.

These reports from Machyn's diary show morris in London to have been a fairly small component within large-scale events.

1553

A Mayday civic procession in Gloucester:
"To those persons that danced the moorys dance   5s."

    The second half of the sixteenth century also sees morris as a minor element within civic and guild processions in a number of provincial towns, but the great bulk of the references come from three towns only, Salisbury, Plymouth and Chester. Only in Salisbury is there any significant continuation beyond 1600.

1555

May Games at St Martin-in-the-Fields in London on 26 May included giants, hobby-horse, drums and guns with morris-dancers and other minstrels.

1557

May Games at Fenchurch Street in London on 30 May included drums and guns and pikes, nine worthies and speeches, morris dance, sultan, elephant with castle, young morens with targets and darts and the Lord and Lady of the May.
    [In case this is all beginning to sound too much like a modern carnival show, it is worth reminding ourselves that there were major differences between then and now. The day before this jolly May Game, Machyn's diary reports four heads set up on London Bridge and their sixteen quarters set up, three and two, on every gate of London – mind the drips as you go through!]

1559

Another Machyn entry, 21 March, tells the usual tale of drums and guns, but ends up with the interesting comment, " .... and after, the mores dancers went into the court, dancing in many offices". Again, we get an impression of the morris being a bit more self-contained than the other components in the procession. Did they go off and get bookings elsewhere? We don't know, for Machyn's attention was firmly focused on processions.

1562

On 1 May a single dancer came from Little Bytham, Lincolnshire, to visit the Duchess of Suffolk at Grimsthorpe. This morris dancer was paid 2s. (Lowe)
    Another performance in the manner of Arbeau's small boy?

1571

As part of a policy of tightening up proper Christian behaviour, Edmund Grindal, Archbishop of York, issued an injunction which included a useful list of customs that were around at the time.

Inquiries should be made
Whether the minister and churchwardens have suffered any Lords of Misrule, or Summer Lords or Ladies, or any disguised persons, or others, in Christmas, or at May Games or any Morris-dancers or others at rush bearings, or at any other times, to come unreverently into the Church or churchyard, and there to dance, or play any unseemly parts with scoffs, jests, wanton gestures or ribald talk, namely in the time of Common Prayer. And what they be that commit such disorder, or accompany or maintain them?

This text, or others quite similar, were used at visitations across the country for the next sixty years or so and it should perhaps be noticed, yet again, that although the Church clearly did not like these customs, the real antagonism arose only when they came into direct conflict with church property or church services.

1575

An enormous extravaganza of an entertainment was put on at Kenilworth by Robert Dudley, Earl of Leicester, to entertain and impress Queen Elizabeth and to drop hints that he would make her a good husband. One of the hints was a staging of a village bride-ale which included "a lively moris dance, according to the ancient manner: six dancers, Maidmarian, and the fool".

1583

Burton refers to the household accounts of the Kytsons of Hengrave Hall, Suffolk:

"In reward to the morres-dancers, at my master
his return into the country   2s.

1586   Kemp in Denmark – see page 17

1589

W. E. St Lawrence Finney (a barrister of disputed accuracy) in his *Mediaeval Games and Gaderyngs at Kingston upon-Thames*, 1936, gives us:

115

The morris dance had become so popular by the time of the Tudors that when Sir Walter Raleigh sailed for North America to found the colony of Virginia for Queen Elizabeth, he took with him a troop of morris dancers and hobby-horse men, 'to provide pastimes and mery diversions' for the native population over there.

He appears to be quoting from an early source if the spelling of 'mery' is anything to go by, but this source has never been identified.

1589
A dispute is recorded between the Sheriff of Oxford and officials of Banbury town council over an alleged attempt to supress May-poles, Morris-dances, Whitsun-ales, etc. (Chandler)

1598
Oxford. Forrest quotes from the Marquis of Salisbury manuscripts:

The inhabitants assembled on the two Sundays before Ascension Day, and on that day, with drum and shot and other weapons, and men attired in women's apparel, brought into the town a woman bedecked with garlands and flowers named by them the Queen of the May. They also had Morrishe dancers and other disordered and unseemly sports, and intended the next Sunday to continue the same abuses.

The absence of sympathy in this account can probably be attributed with equal measure to an upper-class upbringing and to puritan principles.

(1598) John Stow publication marking events earlier in the century – see page 15.

1600   Kemp's Jig – see page 16

1600 and thereabouts
The first quarter of the seventeenth century was a great time for popular theatre, and playwrights worked overtime to meet the demand. Some of these plays mention morris and a handful actually include a morris dance in the performance. Obviously a certain amount of care needs to be exercised in approaching stage morris, for the playwright was clearly trying to achieve a popular hit show: a careful recording of folk custom was not part of his brief. Further, the nature of the performance would have expanded as the flair of the actor/dancers drew reaction from their audience. None of this can be seen in a surviving text. On the other hand

there had to be enough familiarity between the performance and the real world to carry the audience along.

As a rather broad generality it might be said that rising costs had brought an end to the large-scale processions and mayings, and puritan antagonism had hit the smaller, countryside morris events; so, by the early 1600s, the only surviving morris was to be found in the urban theatres, performed by professionals. Of course, out of this background came that best-known morris event of all time, Will Kemp's Nine Day's Wonder.

In most cases morris was introduced into the play format by writing in, as an interlude, a maygame and morris in which the clowns of the company presented an entertainment before the actors representing the gentry, after which the 'gentry' responded with refreshments and cash. This wittingly or unwittingly gathered together ideas of the old Italian intermezzi; the fun and games of the rustic and rural peasant; the formal presentation of an entertainment to a social superior, as in a court masque, and, of course, the duty of the wealthy to be generous to the poor. This was a pretty good attempt by the playwright to win universal appeal, and an explanation of why the same idea was used over and over again.

It is interesting to note, in passing, that theatre itself was a fairly new idea at the time. If we take 'theatre' to mean a group of actors who commissioned and performed plays regularly and lived off the box-office receipts, together with a building that would welcome anybody for the price of an entry ticket, then this all began in London in 1576 with the opening of the 'Theater' in Shoreditch. (Glynne Wickham, *Early English Stages*, 1981.)

1603   Court entertainment – see page 90

Circa 1608

At a somewhat hazy date somewhere between 1605 and 1612 Robert Dover revived the Olympic Games in a large open space on a hill just outside Chipping Campden, Gloucestershire. These games were a celebration of country sports and a blow against the rising tide of puritanism. Held annually, they ran for three days in Whit week and covered a huge range of competitions from chess and skittles to football and cock-fighting, with leaping, wrestling and racing on foot or on hoof. Ideas of the Olympic festivals of ancient Greece mixed with the Cotswold Whitsun Ale made an enormously successful event enjoyed by the whole range of society: even King James showed interest and support. Dover's Games lasted for two hundred and forty years. (Information from Roy Dommett's typescript *Captain Robert Dover's Olympick Games* in Cecil Sharp House.)

There is no specific mention of morris dancing in the early days but it is not difficult to see these Games as a splendid opportunity for dancers in later years to meet, to compete and to collect some money. Many, indeed most, people would agree that the 'Cotswold' of the nineteenth century was the high point of morris dancing so far as personal skill and variety of step and figure can be measured. It was in the Cotswold fairs that the dancers refined this skill, and the Cotswold fairs grew out of Dover's Olympick Games.

1609   Masque – see page 91

1609   *Old Meg of Herefordshire* – see page 18

1613

At a town show in Wells, Somerset, there were three fanciful tableaux strongly reminiscent of Italian theatricals, each including a morris dance: that presented by the Mercers was "A Morrice dance of young children". (Forrest)

1618

King James was clearly concerned by the hardening puritan attitudes, and so he issued *The King's Majesties Declaration to his Subjects concerning Lawfull Sports to be Used* (commonly known as the *Book of Sports*) with the requirement that it be read in parishes.

> Our pleasure likewise is, that after the end of divine service, our good people be not disturbed, letted, or discouraged from any lawful recreation such as dancing, either men or women, archery for men, leaping, vaulting, or any other such harmless recreation, nor from having May-games, Whitsun Ales, and Morris-dances, and the setting up of May-poles and other sports therewith used ....

Under James and Charles the *Book of Sports* remained legally in force until civil war made it irrelevant.

Circa 1633

Richard Baxter the theologian, writing in 1671, lamented the time of his youth and the loss of godly teachers who had been dismissed after refusing to read the *Book of Sports* to their congregations. He went on to recall how the noise of pipe and tabor used to distract Sunday prayers. "And sometimes the Morrice-Dancers would come into the church in all their linen and scarfs and antick dresses with morrice-bells jingling at their legs." (He lived at Eaton Constantine, near Much Wenlock.)

1633

We now come to one of the most awkward entries of this set: the Perth Glovers' dance. It is awkward because we have unusually good descriptions of both the costume and the form of the dance, but there is really nothing else quite like it: it is like a piece in a jigsaw that comes from somebody else's puzzle. It also brings us face to face with the awkward question, are sword dances and morris dances both members of the same family? Should sword dance be included under the morris umbrella?

The story starts with a single costume held first by the Glovers' Hall and now by the Perth Museum and Art Gallery, which long tradition asserts was worn by one of the participants in the 1633 Glovers' dance. Details of this costume were supplied to Sir Walter Scott for his *Fair Maid of Perth*, and a review of a dramatised performance in 1828 refers to "The identical dress of one of the morris-dancers who figured before Charles I". Up to this point nobody had mentioned 'morris', the original performance had always been referred to as a sword dance.

The costume consists of a tunic made up from a bodice of silk dyed green, and a calf-length skirt of undyed silk. Associated with this tunic are twenty-one leather bell-pads, each with a dozen morris-type bells, which could well be contemporary with the costume. A heavily tasselled cap, although much modified, just might retain elements from 1633. A dress sword, once shown as part of this exhibit and dating from about 1800, certainly never appeared before Charles I. It should be noted that this costume was worn at several public celebrations during the Victorian period and picked up oddments like shoes and a ruff along the way. For full details refer to Helen Bennett's article in *Costume*, No. 19, 1985.

Bill Banbury, in an article 'The Morris in Scotland' (*The Morris Dancer*, No. 11, November 1981) quotes from the Glovers' minute book for July 1633:

Thirteen of our brethren of this our calling of Glovers with green caps, silver strings, red ribbons, white shoes and bells about their legs, shearing rappers in their hands and all other equipment, danced our sword dance with many difficult knots and allapallyesse [*à la Paillasse*, in the manner of a clown?], five being under and five above upon their shoulders, three of them dancing through their feet and about them, drinking wine and breaking glasses.

If we add that this was a performance to welcome King Charles I and that it took place on a platform floating on the River Tay, we are a bit lost for words.

The 'scheiring raperis' in the text is all too easily translated as 'shearing rappers' and the modern dancer will have an immediate picture of the flexible steel blade with a handle at both ends as used today by rapper sword dancers, and the use of the words 'many difficult knots' in the minute book lends some support to this view. But 'scheiring' seems to mean having a sharp edge, and a hilt-and-point dance with sharp-edged swords seems too dangerous to contemplate. It is also worth emphasising that all we have here is one instant snapshot of a figure from a dance that must have lasted some significant time – it was, after all, a major item in a royal entertainment. The Perth Glovers' Dance is a fascinating curiosity, but any general conclusions are best avoided.

And what of the relationship between sword and morris? From Cecil Sharp onwards, sword dance groups have been included in morris functions, so there is a modern unity at organisational level, but I feel that in an historical sense there is little to link the two and no real advantage is to be had by treating them together.

1636

> " …. for wassaillers and Morris dancers   5s."

> And in 1660:

> "Given to the Morris dancers   6d."

Very ordinary entries in the household account books of the Barrington family of Hatfield Broad Oak in Essex, until you realise that the Barringtons were Puritans.

1644

The Rump Parliament orders all may-poles to be taken down and removed. (Tollet)

1646

By way of relaxation from the war, a group of Cavaliers were entertained at Witney Wakes and morris was part of that entertainment.

> Some 6 or 7 country fellows with napkins and scarfs and ribbons tied about them and bells at their knees, according to the manner of that sport, and with them a Maid Marian and two fools who fell a-dancing and capering. (Chandler, *Ribbons, Bells*)

Circa 1648

Close by St Paul's Cathedral in London, at 36, Old Change, there stood an inn called the 'Three Morris Dancers' from about 1648 until it was pulled down in 1801 (all dates are vague). During the earlier part of this time it was owned by one John Lisle, a man of whom it was said, rather mysteriously:

> "The man that these Three Morris Dancers owns,
> Is, tho a Welshman, none of Merlin's Sons."

John Lisle seems to have owned a second inn, also called the 'Three Morris Dancers' in nearby Aldersgate Street from the 1660s to 1672. An inn called the 'Three Morris Dancer's described as being in St Martin's-le-Grand from around 1715 to the 1720s could have been the same pub.

The building in Old Change bore a sculptured stone sign picturing three morris dancers, two male and one female. The sign itself does not survive but there are illustrations of it in *The Mirror of Literature* Vol XXIX (1837) p.281 and in *The History of Signboards* by Larwood and Holten, 1867.

It was common practice among traders in the latter half of the seventeenth century to issue their own token coins in order to ease the shortage of official copper money and to help with a bit of advertising. John Lisle issued ha'penny and farthing tokens of this type, probably in the 1660s (numismatic reference, Williamson 2133 and 2134). The legend on the ha'penny reads:

> IOHN LISLE AT THE 3 [illustration of three figures dancing]
> IN THE OLD CHAINGE HIS HALF PENY I L A
> (initials for John Lisle and his wife 'A —-')

1652

Wiltshire Quarter Sessions recorded the morris:
> "Very drunk and disorderly, going in a warlike manner to Pewsey."

The years 1652 and 1655 each provide us with three records of legal action against morris dancers, a concentration which is quite unusual. But then the times were unusual: the King had been executed and Cromwell was in charge. Neither the Puritan movement nor the Church hierarchy could see any justification for morris dancing, and so it would not be much of an exaggeration to think of the morris as being squeezed out of their home village community and turned into roving outlaws.

1660

Tuesday, 29 May – Restoration. Charles II, crossing Blackheath, was met by "a kind of rural triumph expressed by the country swains in a morris dance with the old music of taber and pipe, which was performed with all agility and cheerfulness imaginable". (Chandler, *Ribbons, Bells*)

We may well imagine celebrations to be widespread at this time and morris to be a frequent element within them. At Richmond, in Yorkshire, there were "Two companies of morris dancers who acted their parts to the satisfaction of all spectators". Later, they went on to "act their parts" with a group of sixty nymphs from an adjacent part of the procession (*Gentleman's Magazine*, vol 82, 1812).

Forrest suggests that morris dancers at the Restoration enjoyed a bit of a flash in the pan – "almost as if they were a sentimental memory of earlier times", only to be followed by rapid decay. I prefer the view that, after the antagonism of the Commonwealth and the excitement of the Restoration were over, morris lost its newsworthyness and fell back to its normal and unrecorded position in seventeenth-century village life (whatever that was).

1661

On the first Mayday of the Restoration, a great maypole was erected in the Strand. In two parts, it was 134 feet high according to Hone, and morris dancers with purple scarves danced round about. It was probably replaced in 1713, and four years after that, this replacement was sold to Sir Isaac Newton, who took it to Wanstead and used it to raise the largest telescope in the world.

1663

At seven or eight o'clock in the evening of the first of May, Samuel Pepys was making his way homeward when:

> "In my way in Leadenhall Street there was morris dancing, which I have not seen a great while."

1679   Kirtlington Lamb Ale – see page 20

1686

Like the Perth Glovers' Dance, the Abbot's Bromley Horn Dance is unique and an oddity, but unlike the Glovers' Dance it has never been called morris, so I am cheating somewhat by including it here.

A Keeper of the Ashmolean Museum, Robert Plot, published *The Natural History of Staffordshire* in 1686 and in it he describes a hobby-horse dance.

The hobby-horse was in fact an ancillary character with a board cut-out horse between his legs and a bow and arrow designed to make a noise and not release the arrow. There were six dancers, each carrying on his shoulders a reindeer's head (with antlers), three painted white and three red with the arms of the chief local families on the palms. "They danced the heys and other country dances." Cakes and ale were available to reward those giving pennies and the money went to the repair of the church and the support of the poor.

1688

The account books of the Glovers' Company in Shrewsbury show payment of one shilling to the 'Bedlam-Morris', and in the following year five shillings to 'the Bedloms' (Heaney, *Bedlam Morris*, 1985). The word 'bedlam' is rare in morris before the 1970s revival: it presumably refers to behaviour reminiscent of the madhouse, although Heaney has suggested that 'Bedlam Morris' might identify a particular style of performance somewhat different from that at the Whitsun Ales.

1702

Celia Fiennes described the coronation procession for Queen Anne on 23rd April, in Bath. Of one element in a large procession, she wrote:

> Next followed four couple of maurice dancers with their prancing horses, in holland shirts with laced hats ribboned, and cross swashes and garters with bells, with their two antiques dressed in their formalities, with handkerchiefs in their hands dancing all the way.

1705

At a celebration to mark the laying of the foundation stone for Blenheim Palace, three teams of morris dancers performed, 'one of young fellows, one of maidens, and one of old beldames'. (Chandler)

1712

Little Crosby in Lancashire. Nicholas Blundell's *Diary and Letter Book* from the years 1702 to 1728 gives one of the best early descriptions of the way ceremonial dance was fitted into the round of agricultural labour. It is so useful, in fact, that I include it here, notwithstanding the fact that it tells of a sword dance rather than morris.

Marl is a natural mix of clay and lime which was dug out, carted and spread on the fields to revive fertility every twenty years or so. In 1712, Blundell decided the time was right; he located a suitable source of marl and set up a contract for the labour. Nineteen men worked from 3am until late, shifting around eight hundred cart loads a day. The neighbours came to watch. This heavy labour was relieved by generous food and drink and some entertainment.

> "July 3rd. I made a sword dance against my marlpit is flowered."

I take this to mean he devised or updated a sword dance to be performed at a celebration to be held in the marlpit.

> July 7th. I was very busy most of the afternoon shaping tinsel etc for the garland of my new marlpit, and after supper the women helped to paste some things for it. I began to teach the eight sword dancers their dance which they are to dance at the flowering of my marlpit. Dr Cawood played to them.
>
> July 8th. I was very busy making caps etc for my marlers and dancers, several of Great Crosby lasses helped me. The young women of this town, Moorhouses and Great Crosby dressed the garlands in my barn. I taught my eight sword dancers their dance, they had music and danced it in my barn.
>
> July 9th. I was extremely busy all morning making some things to adorn my marlers heads. My marlpit was flowered very much to the satisfaction of the spectators, all the fourteen marlers had a particular dress upon their heads and carried each of them a musket or gun. The six garlands etc were carried by young women in procession, the eight sword dancers went along with them to the marlpit where they danced, the music was Gerald Holrold and his son, and Richard Tatlock, at night they danced in the barn.
>
> (Edited Margaret Blundell, 1952)

On 23 July, finishing day, they fetched home the maypole from the pit and had sword dancing and a merry night with the neighbours in the Hall and in the barn.

Two years later Nicholas Blundell reports seeing morris dancers going their round in order to rear a maypole at Sefton.

1716   Whitsun Ales – see page 7

1730s

Keith Chandler notes that in this decade there were active sets of morris dancers at Aynho, Brackley, Kirtlington, Middleton Cheney, Northleach, Somerton, Turweston and Croughton (*Ribbons, Bells*). All are villages in the

South Midlands – Oxfordshire, Gloucestershire, Northamptonshire and Buckinghamshire (the area of Chandler's study, often called, more loosely, the Cotswolds).

Even without going into the details of the records, we are beginning to get first sight of a pattern that will be familiar to all present-day dancers: a substantial number of villages, scattered widely across the Cotswolds, each being the base for a morris side having some degree of permanence or continuity (and not just assembled for a particular occasion). Sides that travelled to grand houses and to other villages would be met by the question 'Where d'you come from?' They would then become known as the morris dancers that came from Brackley, or wherever.

So, one answer to that question, "How old is it?" could be, "Two hundred and seventy years".

1744

The *Gloucester Journal* announced a competition on the Tuesday of Whit week 1744 to be held at the 'Swan', Coln St Aldwyn. "Six exceeding good knots [of ribbons] to be morrice-danced for." (Chandler)

1747

The *Northampton Mercury* announced a performance by the famous Blakesley Morrice at the 'Black Swan', Great Brington, in September of 1747 as one of the attractions of the annual hiring fair. (Chandler)

These two entries illustrate that the mutually beneficial relationship between morris dancers and pubs was already well established and it is also noteworthy that the weekly provincial newspapers, which were fairly new on the scene at this time, were serving both to advertise morris events in their own day, and also to preserve records for the present-day researcher.

1749

Morris tours have been disrupted by a wide variety of calamities, but this is the only case I know involving an earthquake.

The *Lincoln, Rutland and Stamford Mercury* of 6 January 1750 reported that, on Innocents' Day in the afternoon (28 December), a morris side from Grimsby was making its way from Laceby to Alesby when

> They felt two such terrible shocks of the earth that they had much ado to hold their feet and thought the ground was ready to swallow them up, whereupon, thinking that God was angry at them for playing the fool, they returned immediately to Laceby in a great fright and the next day home, not daring to pursue their intended circuit and dancing.
> (Sue Swift, *Morris Matters* Vol 7 No 1)

I am reminded of the morris side from Blackwell in Warwickshire who gave up dancing in 1867 after their musician was struck by lightning. But I digress. The significant point to notice here is the distance between Grimsby and the Cotswolds. For many reasons morris research has concentrated on the Cotswold area, and so it is good to note that, one hundred and fifty miles away, morris dancers were going out on a walking tour of local villages in much the same way.

1774

A procession organised by a newly-elected Knight of the Shire travelled from Wotton to Aylesbury. It included "a very large band of music, several flags, and a Morris, dancing all the way" (Chandler). Morris was clearly an acceptable entertainment in the world of county politics.

1777

A dispute arose between the adjacent villages of Eccles and Barton upon Irwell in Lancashire over a marl pit, and this led to competitive guisings and money collection. Though billed as a war, I think we may take it that this was a light-hearted romp. With some in fancy dress, they went round the two villages "with drums beating, colours flying, trumpets sounding, music playing and about sixteen couples of morris dancers". (Harland and Wilkinson, *Lancashire Legends*, 1873)

This is not the most reliable of records, but if the date and the thirty-two dancers are correct, then it conveniently matches our present-day ideas of the processional dances from Lancashire, and it is clearly different from the six-man sets of further south.

1781

The *Torrington Diaries* of John Byng record on 3 June,

> "During our short stay at Wallingford a set of morris dancers pranced away in the street; these, with other old rural sports, I feared had been lost."

1783

A much repeated item from Waldron's completion of Jonson's *Sad Shepherd* tells of a company of morris dancers from Abingdon seen dancing at Richmond in Surrey. The dancers and the fool were "Berkshire husbandmen taking an annual circuit".

A number of authors have pointed to the large population of horses in London and the consequent need for extensive hayfields nearby, to be followed by a peak in the labour requirement at hay-making time. It is suggested that agricultural workers came up to London for the hay-making and that some of them made a bit of money on the side by morris dancing in the streets.

1785

The Whitsun Ale was last kept at Greatworth, Northamptonshire, in 1785 and the order of the procession gives us some idea of the rustic formality of the occasion.

Constable.

Esquire or Lord's Son.

Fool,

attired in a motley garb, with a gridiron painted
or worked with a needle on his back,

carrying a stick with bladder
and calf's tail.

My Lord's music.   My Lady's music.

Majordomo, and his Lady as Queen of the May.

Supporters on each side.

My Lord's morris

(six in number).

Butler.   Butler

Treasurer,   Treasurer,

with sash and box,   with sash and box.

The whole decorated with badges of orange and blue.

A maypole with garlands was fixed up for the merry company to dance around, and the morris dancers, with the grimaces and gesticulations of the Fool, added to the hilarity of the assembled multitude. A barn was prepared for the banquetting; and all those who misconducted themselves were obliged to ride a wooden horse, and if they were still more unruly, they were put into the stocks, which was termed 'being My Lord's organist'.

(Anne Baker, *Glossary of Northamptonshire Words*, 1854)

Miss Baker goes on to suggest that, although the Whitsun Ales had come to an end, the slot in the calendar was often taken over for the annual procession and feast of a Friendly Society.

1790

A letter signed 'Durgan' in the *Gentleman's Magazine* Vol 60 tells of 'Furry Day' held on 8 May in Helston, Cornwall. After a morning spent in noisy revelry, about midday they start to dance hand in hand round the streets (called a 'Faddy'). In the afternoon the gentility go off for refreshments, "and return in a morrice-dance to the town where they form a Faddy and dance through the streets till it is dark, claiming a right of going through any persons house, in at one door and out at the other".

What Durgan meant by a morrice-dance is, of course, quite uncertain.

1790s

Chandler confirms teams in the Oxfordshire and Buckinghamshire villages of Bicester Kings End, Burford, Marsh Gibbon, Newton, Shalstone, Twyford and Westbury. (*Ribbons, Bells*)

1792

The *Star* of 9 August records that:

On Monday July 30th the morris dancers of Pendleton (Lancashire) paid their annual visit to Salford. They were adorned with all the variety of colours that a profusion of ribbons could give them, and had a very showy garland.

A fifty-mile round trip seems a bit unlikely for those days, so I suspect Pendleton should be Pendlebury, four miles from Salford.

1798

An ancient custom in Lichfield, Staffordshire, included a Whitsun procession to the Greenhill Bower. Stebbing Shaw, in his *History and Antiquities of Staffordshire 1798*, noted that the high constables of the city were led in the procession by eight morrice dancers and a fool, fantastically dressed: these dancers went on to attend the constables during their tour of the town's wards and later on they took a place in the evening procession.

Circa 1800

In her *Glossary of Northamptonshire Words*, 1854, Anne Baker reports the last celebration of a Whitsun Ale at King's Sutton, Northamptonshire, "about the commencement of the present century".

The morris dancers were dressed with cross-belts of broad ribbon ornamented with five roses before, five behind, and one on each shoulder, with bunches of blue and red ribbon at each hip.

Circa 1805

Douce, 1807, notes that "a very few years since" a company of morris dancers "was seen at Usk in Monmouthshire, which was attended by a boy Maid Marian, a hobby-horse, and a fool. They professed to have kept up the ceremony at that place for the last three hundred years." A familiar story, but not necessarily one to be believed.

1817

On 12 June, eight morris dancers with bells and staves were seen in St James's Street, London, with the music of pipe and tabor: their dances were noted as pleasingly varied and well performed. "This ancient pastime may be held a rare sight." (*Gentleman's Magazine*).

1817

Ormerod's *History of Cheshire*, 1819, tells of rushcart processions as in use at Lymm, 1817, where "The cart thus loaded goes round to the neighbouring seats, preceded by male and female morris dancers".

1819

A letter marked 'E.H., West Glamorgan' in the *Gentleman's Magazine* of 1819 describes 'The Merry Dancers' who go from door to door at Christmas time: usually three dancers with short jackets and hats decorated with a profusion of paper ornaments. They dance heys and setting, then two go into a spin. The music is generally a harp, although the fiddle is creeping in. These are probably the 'Three Merry Dancers of Wales' referred to elsewhere and look very like ancestors of what we now call 'Border Morris'.

1822

A letter signed 'W.S. Wickenden' in the *Gentleman's Magazine* described the "Whitsuntide amusement of morris dancing" at Blakeney, Gloucestershire, on the edge of the Forest of Dean.

"They literally cover their bodies and hats with ribbons of all colours and, preceded by two persons bearing a flag and two rusty swords, a Tom Fool (as they call him), and a Maid Marian, they cut the most ridiculous capers and contortions."

Wickenden offers the thought that "the more grotesque the dress and actions of the dancers are, the more near they resemble the ancient dance".

Do we have here a man who had seen the fifteenth-century engravings and was adjusting what he saw, to match what he thought he ought to see?

1823

A French author, A. Pichot, visited a fair at Brook Green (beside the Hammersmith Flyover in West London) and saw:

> A group of young rustics, attired in dresses at once remarkable for elegance and simplicity and decorated with numerous bows of ribbon. They had small jingling bells fastened to their knees and ankles. Some waved white handkerchiefs and others wands. They advanced in a regular step, forming a kind of graceful dance and keeping time by striking their wands one against another. (Quoted by Chandler, *Ribbons, Bells*)

Without wishing to be too contentious: here was a Frenchman who didn't know what he was supposed to see, reporting what he actually saw, and producing a description that will sound very familiar to anyone with a working knowledge of Cotswold.

Circa 1824

Spelsbury in Oxfordshire acquired a certain fame, following twentieth century arguments as to whether women could, couldn't, should, shouldn't dance morris in general, and Cotswold in particular. For Spelsbury is the only village we know that had a regularly performing all-female morris side.

John Corbett of Spelsbury (when aged 88) was interviewed by a collector in 1894 and said that about seventy years ago there was a set of women morris dancers who used to dance on Whit Monday: girls of eighteen to twenty, they were under the escort of a man who looked after them. They wore head-dresses of ribbons and flowers, short skirts, bells on their legs (same as the men) and carried white handkerchiefs. With them went a clown or 'squire' with bladder and cow's tail and a man playing pipe and tabor. One day they danced on the top of the church tower. (From the Manning manuscripts.)

Spelsbury also had a separate team of male morris dancers and occasionally the two sides went out together.

1825

A letter to Hone's *Year Book* dated 4 May 1825 from Jesse Lee of Rochdale gives the format of a rushcart procession in Lancashire. Men with whips which they crack to clear the way are followed by a number of men with horse-bells about them jumping grotesquely and jingling the bells. The band follows and then, sometimes, a number of young men as morris dancers, followed by young women bearing garlands and, lastly, the cart. (This letter is reproduced in Burton, 1891.)

1826

Three sightings of morris dancers were reported from the streets of London this year. No doubt, more haymakers.

> Though the streets were dirty and the rain fell reluctantly, yet they heeded not the elemental warfare, but danced and smiled, and danced and smiled again. (Hone, 1827)

1828

A description of preparations for the Whitsun Ale at Milton-under-Wychwood in Jackson's *Oxford Journal* of 24 May 1828, marks a start of the sticky romanticism that adheres to so many public festivals of the Victorian period, and which left traces well into the twentieth century.

> And Ceres, from her bounteous hoard, has selected the finest flour to be made into rich cakes for the fair, and to be carried away with triumphant joy by the sprightly morris dancers.

1830

Fanny Kemble, the well-known actress, wrote a letter on 7 September describing a chance encounter with a rush-bearing at Heaton, Lancashire, "which greatly delighted me". The horse-drawn rush-cart led the procession on this occasion, "After this came twelve country lads and lasses dancing the real old morris dance, their handkerchiefs flying, in all the rustic elegance of apparel they could command for the occasion." A band followed, then Adam and Eve covered with finery, and in conclusion a fool with a bladder on a stick. (See her *Record of a Girlhood*, 1878.)

Circa 1834

Correspondence in the *Birmingham Weekly Post* of 1884 told that, about fifty years ago, outdoor workers and boatmen kept out of work by severe frost danced a stick dance beside the canal to the tune of a fiddle (Heaney, *edlam Morris*). I recall a similar event along the River Severn when morris dancers were referred to as 'The Unemployed'. The recovery of morris dancing in the 1930s into an upper-middle-class society made little mention of the importance morris once had for keeping body and soul together.

Circa 1836

Nobody would dispute that the morris side from Bampton, Oxfordshire, has the longest and most complete history of any group still dancing today. Chandler notes that the earliest remembered dancer, Charles Tanner, born 1816, was likely to have started dancing when he was twenty years of age. We might therefore see 1836 as the earliest point at which morris makes contact with living memory.

1837

The author of the article in *The Mirror of Literature*, while making his enquiries about the 'Three Morris Dancers' pub (see item under 1648 above) met by chance "a company of May-day sweeps in all their sooty glory, which has made us suspect the partial, if not entire, identity of the morris dance and the sweeps' Saturnalia".

Before 1840

One curious fact about morris distribution is the influence of the River Thames: there are books-full of material recorded north of the Thames, but nothing south of it. (I speak here of what we might call traditional times, say 1660 – 1900). Well, almost nothing. George Frampton wrote an article for *Morris Matters*, 1979, called 'Morris in Hampshire' in which the best he could find was "at Farnborough before 1840, when a party of eight men besides a fiddler made two sets of four-handed reels". A reference to 'clattering dancers' suggests to me either heavy boots, or clashing sticks.

Simple reel dances are fairly widespread, both in the social dance world and under the 'morris' banner. Headington Quarry has a reel, so does Steeple Claydon, Buckinghamshire, and reels lie at the heart of most Border morris dances.

1844

The Duke of Buckingham held a celebration at Stowe to mark the coming of age of his son the Marquis of Chandos. Dinner was served to 2,400 and afterwards there were rustic sports, with two companies of morris dancers who danced alternately. A watercolour was painted of the scene, and this was reproduced on the cover of *English Dance and Song*, Sept/Oct 1957. The

Duke had been very keen to revive morris in the villages on his estate (where, it seems, morris dancing had been popular thirty or forty years before) and to this end he had ordered a dozen sets of morris kit to be made at his own expense. He seemed to believe that morris dancing would reduce the amount of time that the young lads were spending in the beer-houses. (Taken from press reports in the above mentioned copy of *ED&S.*) With this degree of gentry sponsorship, one is left to wonder how many changes to style, attitude and costume were introduced into the dance. But then, morris has always responded to outside forces: that's why it is still with us.

1846

A newspaper report of the Buxton Well Dressing of 1846 is quoted in Brand, 1854.

> About two o'clock the morris dancers started on their round accompanied by the Duke of Devonshire's and the Pilsley bands, but their graceful evolutions were frequently interrupted by showers of rain.

1847

John Gutch, in his *Lytell Geste of Robin Hode*, 1847, notes that in Droitwich, Worcestershire, on 27 June,

> a large party of morris dancers still continue to parade the town and neighbourhood, it is said, in commemoration of a discovery of some extensive salt mines.

1848

The *Oxford Chronicle* of 24 June reported on the Kirtlington Lamb Ale, giving a rather sad picture of decline: the green had been enclosed and cottages destroyed; most of the attractions were still there, but attendances had been falling off for some years. (Chandler)

1849

A first-hand account of morris dancing before 1850, written by someone who was a member of the team, is rare indeed. So, to round off this chapter of 'What Actually Happened', I quote from a letter, signed T.W. Luker, published in the *Birmingham Weekly Post* of 6 September 1884. (Chandler adds the information that Thomas W. Luker was born in 1842.)

> I was born in a large village bordering on Oxfordshire and Gloucestershire, called Filkins, where every lad at six years of age

understood morris dances: it was more noted for them than any other village I ever heard of.— They used to practise all the year round but they began business in earnest on what is known as Holy Thursday, about nine days before Whitsuntide, and they used to travel for about six weeks for thirty miles round – six dancers and clown with calf's tail on a stick and a bladder on the end. The company I refer to had for musician a man with no use in his legs, who could play the violin admirably: and what makes my memory so good is, I used to push his carriage and to beat a small tambourine. Although it is thirty-five years ago I well remember that the money used to flow in for the first three weeks of the season in a most extraordinary way. Their dress was chiefly white knee breeches (with bells hidden from view) in [with?] various colours of silk strapped round their legs, and ribbons of many colours on their arms, and a sash of broad ribbon round their shoulders with a bow under their left arm. Their steps were called 'Facing Up' and 'Side Step', and mostly going round shaking the right leg in a crooked position, and clapping of hands both behind and before was much resorted to, and they were noted for what was called jig dancing single handed. Although it is many years ago I remember many of the names of the tunes such as 'Sally Clack' and 'Highland Mary'. And if I was a man of music I could instruct a company now in many of the dances.

(This letter was reproduced in *English Dance and Song* Vol. 42 No. 3.)

CHAPTER 6: MAIN CHRONOLOGICAL SEQUENCE
Summary

* Marks the events that have already been mentioned in the text of Chapters 1 to 5.

HFA Refers to numbers allocated to events in Heaney and Forrest, *Annals of Early Morris* (1991)

Date	Key Words	Page	HFA	Country if not in England
1137	Lérida	94		Spain
1240	* Summer Game	70		
1306	* Summer Game	84		Scotland
1334	* Mumming	83		
1341	Petrarch	95		Italy
1343	* Tournament	78		
1344	*The Romance of Alexander*	96		Belgium
1347	* Disguising	78		
1375	* Tournament	78		
1377	* Mumming	80		
1389	* Entry into Paris	75		France
1389	Entry into Paris	97		France
1391	* King of Fools	74		
1392	'The Burning Ballet'	98		France
1418	* Mumming	83		
c.1427	John Lydgate	99		
1432	* Entry into London	76		
1438	*Liber Particularis*	100		Italy
1440	Gilles de Rais	101		France
1454	* Entremet	73		France
1457	* Rogationtide procession	86		
1457	Entertainment at Tours	102		France
1458	*Knight of the Swan*	103		France
1458	Will of Wetenhale	103	1	
1458	Will of Chaworth	104	2	
1459	Entertainment at Tours	104		France
1459	*Jehan de Saintré*	105		France

Date	Key Words	Page	HFA	Country if not in England
1466	Household accounts	106	3	
1467	Salt	106		France
1468	* Entremet, Tournament	73 and 78		Belgium
1469	* Summer Game	84		
1473	Italian theatricals	106		Italy
1477	Civic London	107	4	
1491	* Italian theatricals	87		Italy
1494	Court	107	5	
c.1500	*Dance of Fools*	107		Denmark
1501	* Court disguising	79	7	
1501	Court	108	6 & 7	
1502	Court	108	9	
1502	* Italian theatricals	88		Italy
1502	Scottish Court	108	10	Scotland
1504	Scottish Court	108	12	Scotland
c.1505	William Dunbar	109	13	Scotland
1507	Civic London	109	15	
1507	Kingston-upon-Thames	109	14	
1509	* Italian theatricals	88		Italy
1510	Will of Jackson	109	21	
1510	Court	110		
1511	Court pageant	110	23	
1512	Scottish Court	110	26 & 27	Scotland
1513	* Italian theatricals	88		Italy
1514	Court interlude	110	30	
1517	Corpus Christi	111		Portugal
1521	Civic London	111	40 & 41	
1522	Court disguising	112	50	
1525	Civic London	112	52 & 55	
1526	Sandwich disorder	112	60	
1532	Salt	113	70	
c.1535	* Disguising	89 and 90		
c.1540	* Arbeau's small boy	15		France
1541	Civic London	113	84	
1552	Civic London	113	92 & 93	
1553	Civic London	113	95	
1553	Civic Gloucester	114	97	

Date	Key Words	Page	HFA	Country if not in England
1555	Civic London	114	100	
1557	Civic London	114	104	
1559	Civic London	114	106	
1562	Single dancer	114	116	
1571	Church injunction	115	144	
1575	Court extravaganza	115	153	
1583	Household accounts	115	186	
1586	* Kemp in Denmark	17		Denmark
1589	Walter Raleigh	115	B17	U.S.A.
1589	Civic Oxford	116	213?	
1598	Civic Oxford	116	282	
(1598)	* John Stow publication	15	279	
1600	* Kemp's Jig	16	304-315	
c.1600	Theatre	116		
1603	* Court entertainment	90	338	
c.1608	Dover's Games	117		
1609	* Masque	91		
1609	* *Old Meg of Herefordshire*	18	375	
1613	Civic Wells	118	398	
1618	*Book of Sports*	118	423	
c.1633	Morris/Church conflict	118	662	
1633	Perth Glovers' dance	119	B25	Scotland
1636	Household accounts	120	535 & 606	
1644	Maypoles	120		
1646	Village sports	120	560	
c.1648	'Three Morris Dancers' pub	121	329	
1652	Law court	121	572	
1660	Restoration	122	602 & 603	
1661	Maypoles	122	610	
1663	Pepys	122	640	
1679	* Kirtlington Lamb Ale	20	678	
1686	Abbot's Bromley	122		
1688	Civic Shrewsbury	123	693 & A41	
1702	Coronation procession	123	707	
1705	Blenheim Palace	123	712	
1712	Marlpit flowering	123	734 & 731	
1716	* Whitsun ales	7	736	

Date	Key Words	Page	HFA	Country if not in England
1730s	Morris in the Cotswolds	124	769 etc.	
1744	Morris in the Cotswolds	125	792	
1747	Morris in the Cotswolds	125	797	
1749	Earthquake	125		
1774	Civic procession	126		
1777	Morris in Lancashire	126		
1781	Morris in the Cotswolds	126		
1783	Morris on tour	126		
1785	Whitsun ale	127		
1790	Helston Furry Day	128		
1790s	Morris in the Cotswolds	128		
1792	Morris in Lancashire	128		
1798	Morris in Staffordshire	128		
c.1800	Whitsun Ale	128		
c.1805	Morris in Monmouthshire	129		
1817	Morris on tour	129		
1817	Cheshire rushcart	129		
1819	Morris in Wales	129		Wales
1822	Morris in the Forest of Dean	129		
1823	Morris on tour	130		
c.1824	Women's morris	130		
1825	Lancashire rushcart	131		
1826	Morris on tour	131		
1828	Whitsun ale	131		
1830	Lancashire rushcart	131		
c.1834	Out of work	131		
c.1836	Living memory, Bampton	132		
1837	London sweeps	132		
Before 1840	South of the Thames	132		
1844	Aristocratic celebration	132		
1846	Buxton Well Dressing	133		
1847	Morris in Worcestershire	133		
1848	Kirtlington Lamb Ale	133		
1849	Morris in Filkins	133		

CHAPTER 7

ACCOUNT BOOK ENTRIES FROM ENGLISH PARISH CHURCHES

If we think of a churchwarden sitting down to make up his accounts, we naturally think of him working with some sort of method. Consequently we might imagine that entries which are nearby on the page are a record of things that were nearby in life. There are obviously some grains of truth in this supposition, but there are no guarantees. Accounts for a parish feast at Kingston mention 'morris garments' in one place and 'bells for the dancers' in another. It seems entirely reasonable to bring these entries together and affirm that the 'garments' and the 'bells' were both worn by morris dancers, but in fact the 'garments' entry makes no mention of dancers, and the 'bells' entry makes no mention of morris. It is also worth wondering whether 'what was written down' is quite the same as 'what we read'. I read a "black morris coat" (Dunmow 1527): the original has "a blakk morres coott", but this could be read as 'a black-a-moor's coat' and have nothing to do with morris.

The account book entries that make up the body of this chapter have been chosen with a fairly severe eye, admitting only those that bear a fairly certain connection with morris dancing. Mere juxtaposition is not enough. There is, however, a partial exception to this rule in the cases where a churchwarden has lumped a variety of things together into the same account book item: if there is one thing in such a group that warrants entry here, then the complete entry has been included.

Original account books are written in a hand that is difficult for a non-specialist to read and so this chapter has been put together using the secondary sources listed below. A small word of warning to anyone cross-checking between these sources: dating in the originals is sometimes by regnal year and sometimes by the term of office of the churchwardens, neither of which starts on 1 January or even on Lady Day. There is therefore room for choice when setting these dates into a calendar form: we need to be aware that one writer's 1536/37 (Burton) may be the same as another writer's 1539 (Lowe): an entry that will be found here under 1537/38.

The Sources

Rev Daniel Lysons, *The Environs of London*, 1792.

Thomas Langley, *The History of the Hundred of Desborough*, 1797.

Rev Charles Coates, *The History of Reading*, 1802.

Rev John Brand, *Observations on Popular Antiquities*, 1841 edition.

J.O. Halliwell, *Dictionary of Archaic and Provincial Words*, 1847.

Rev Charles Kerry, *The History of the Hundred of Bray*, 1861.

Rev Charles Kerry, *A History of the Municipal Church of St Lawrence, Reading*, 1883.

Alfred Burton, *Rush-bearing*, 1891.

Rev J. Charles Cox, *Churchwardens' Accounts*, 1913.

W.E. St Lawrence Finny, *Mediaeval Games and Gaderyngs at Kingston-upon-Thames*, Surrey Archaeological Collections, 1936.

Rev J.E. Farmiloe and Rosita Nixseaman, *Elizabethan Churchwardens' Accounts*, Bedfordshire Historical Record Society, 1953.

E.C. Cawte, Alex Helm, R.J. Marriott and N. Peacock, 'A Geographical Index of the Ceremonial Dance in Great Britain', *JEFDSS*, 1960.

J.R. Smith, 'The Suppression of Pestiferous Dancing in Essex', *English Dance and Song*, Spring 1974.

George Frampton, 'Morris in Hampshire', *Morris Matters*, Autumn 1979.

Matthew Alexander, 'The Morris in Surrey', *The Southern Rag*, Oct–Dec 1979.

The Entries

For early and uncertain entries see page 86.

1507/8	**Kingston-upon-Thames**		(Lysons)
	For painting of the morris garments		
	and for certain great liveries.	2s	4d
	For four plyts and a quarter of lawn		
	for the morris garments.	2s	11d
	For orseden for the same.		10d
	For bells for the dancers.		12d
			(Finny)
	Item paid for meat and drink for		
	the morris dancers on the fair day.		14d
	Item payed for two pairs of shoes		
	for the morris dancers.		14d

['Liveries' are often mentioned but never explained. It seems likely that they were ribbons or badges marking the event: perhaps a sign that the entrance fee had been paid. A 'great livery' might have been a ribbon sash in the colours of the day: ancestor to the tee-shirt. A 'plyt' was a standard piece of lawn fabric and 'orseden' was thin brass sheet.]

1509/10	**Kingston-upon-Thames**			(Lysons)
	For silver paper for the morris dancers.		7d	
				(Cox)
	Paid for meat and drink for			
	the morris dancers.		2d	
	And on Corpus Christi day.		4d	
	For six pairs of shoes for			
	the morris dancers.	4s	0d	
1513	**Reading, St Lawrence**			(Kerry)
	Item paid for a hoop for the giant			
	and for ale to the morris dancers			
	on the Dedication Day.		3d	
1515/16	**Kingston-upon-Thames**			(Finny)
	Shoes for morris dancers and Robin			
	Hood and his company			
	[13 pairs at 8d a pair].			
	Item for making of a crown for			
	the morris dancers.		2d	
	Item for meat and drink for the			
	morris dancers upon fair day.		9d	
	Item in money to young men that took			
	upon them to play the morris dances.		6d	
	Item for a taborer upon fair eve and			
	fair day and for bells for the dancers.		16d	
1519/20	**Kingston-upon-Thames**			(Lysons)
	Shoes for the morris dancers, the Friar			
	and Maid Marian at 7d a pair	5s	4d	
	[Finny amends this item to show eight			
	pairs of shoes at 8d a pair, which			
	fits the total more happily].			
				(Finny)
	Item paid for bells for the			
	morris dancers.	5s	0d	
1521/22	**Kingston-upon-Thames**			(Lysons)
	Eight yards of fustian for the			
	morris dancers' coats.	16s	0d	

141

	A dozen of gold skins for the morris.			10d
	[Presumably gold leaf for gilding			
	or leather already gilded.]			
1527	**Dunmow, Essex**	(Smith)		
	Item paid for a black morris coat.			12d
	[It seems the morris was out			
	on a Corpus Christi tour.]			
1529	**Reading, St Lawrence**	(Kerry)		
	Item for bells for the morris dancers.		3s	6d
	Item for three hats for the morris dancers.			6d
	Item for three yards of buckram for			
	the morris dancers.			12d
1530	**Reading, St Lawrence**	(Kerry)		
	Item for a gross of bells for the morris			
	dancers.		3s	0d
1530	**Guildford, Holy Trinity**	(Alexander)		
	The parish was hiring out morris gear.			
1532	**Dunmow, Essex**	(Smith)		
	Tour on Corpus Christi, including			
	Great Dunmow, Thaxted and Great Easton.			
	Collected	£3	9s	4d
	Expenses		15s	4d
1536/37	**Kingston-upon-Thames**	(Lysons)		
	Five hats and four purses for the dancers.			4½d
		(Finny)		
	Item for half a piece of fustian of gene			
	[green?] for the morris dancers' coats.		7s	5d
	Item for making of the morris dancers'			
	and the Friar's coats.		4s	1d
	Item for seven pairs of leather garters to			
	set the bells upon.			6d
	Item for the costs and charges of the morris			
	dancers as meats and drinks.		3s	8d
	Item paid for washing the			
	morris dancers' coats.			4d

[Coates has 'two hundred dozen of liveries',
which is an impressive figure if these are,
indeed, badges for sale.]

1537/38   **Kingston-upon-Thames**   (Lysons)
Memorandum. Left in the keeping of the wardens now
being – a Friar's coat of russet, and a kirtle of worsted
welted with red cloth; a mowren's coat of buckram, and
four morris dancers' coats of white fustian spangled,
and two green satin coats, and a dysard's coat of cotton,
and six pairs of garters with bells.

1540   **Maldon, Essex**   (Smith)
[This reference is, in fact, from the account books of the
Borough Chamberlain – not from the Churchwardens –
but the function looks to be very similar in this instance.]
Expenses for the play on Sunday 11 July (Relic Sunday)
included:

Paid for . . . . dancers' bells.	4d
Paid to the morris dancers.	8d

1541/42   **Reading, St Lawrence**   (Kerry)

Paid for liveries and painting the morris coats.	11d

1553   **Reading, St Lawrence**   (Kerry)
Debts – Item upon John Saunders, the apparel of the
morris dancers.
He said he delivered them to Mr Buklond.

1554   **Abingdon, St Helen**   (Brand)
Morris bells are mentioned up to 1592.

1557   **Reading, St Mary**   (Coates)

Item paid to the morris dancers and the minstrels, meat and drink at Whitsontide.	3s	4d
Paid to them the Sunday after May-day.		20d
Paid to the painter for painting of their coats.	2s	8d
Paid to the painter for two dozen of liveries.		20d

1558	**Leicester, St Martin**		(Cox)
	Received for the morris dance		
	of the children.	3s	0d

1560	**Abingdon, St Helen**		(Brand)
	For two dozen of morris bells.	1s	0d

1562	**West Tarring, Sussex**		(Cawte and others)
	Mention of morris in the churchwardens' accounts.		

1562/63	**Southampton**		(Frampton)
	To singers, players and morris		
	dancers on May Day.	3s	4d
	[It is not clear whether this is a churchwarden		
	account, or not.]		

1563	**Northill, Bedfordshire**	(Farmiloe and Nixseaman)	
	More for the making of the morris coats.	2s	4d
	More for the morris dancers toward		
	their shoes.	3s	0d
	More for morris bells.	3s	0d
	More for the morris dancers' shoes		
	to Webster.	2s	8d

1565	**Northill, Bedfordshire**	(Farmiloe and Nixseaman)	
	For seven pairs of dancing shoes.	5s	10d
	For morris bells and leather.	8s	6d

1571	**St Giles, Cripplegate – London**		(Halliwell)
	[The parish paid some of the costs of the Lord Mayor's outing.]		
	Item – paid in charges by the appointment of the parishioners, for the setting forth of a giant, morris dancers, with six cavaliers and three boys on horseback to go in the watch before the Lord Mayor upon Midsummer Eve, as may appear by particulars for		
	the furnishing of the same. £6	9s	9d

1571	Archbishop Grindal's Injunction (see Chapter 6).		

c.1575	**Dunmow, Essex**		(Smith)
	[The Borough Chamberlain took over some of the		

Churchwardens' functions around 1555. This is an
entry from the Borough Court Book.]
Item that I received of James Ailet
for the morris dancers   2s   0d

1585   **St Columb Major, Cornwall**   (Cox)
[List of parish goods includes:]
Five coats for dancers, a Friar's coat,
24 dancing bells, a streamer of red
moccado and locram, six yards of
white woollen cloth.
[St Columb Major is only four miles from
Lanherne, see 1466 in Chapter 6.]

1591   **St Mary-at-Hill, London**   (Burton)
Bells for the dancers are charged in the accounts.
[Brand was at one time the incumbent at this church.]

1595   **Great Marlow, Buckinghamshire**   (Cox)
Paid to one for the carrying of the
morris coat to Maidenhead.   4d

1602   **Bray, Berkshire**   (Kerry)
An inventory of church goods remaining
the 24 of June, Anno 1602:
Item four sheets of lead, five garters with
bells, and four morris coats.

1603   **Leicester**   (Cawte and others)
Mention of morris at Whitsun.

1608   **Great Marlow, Buckinghamshire**   (Langley)
[Among the church goods:]
Item – five pairs of garters and bells
Item – five coats and a fool's coat.
Item – four feathers.
[The morris coats were lent out to neighbouring
parishes.]

1612   **Great Marlow, Buckinghamshire**   (Cox)
Received of the churchwardens of Bisham,
loan of our morris coats and bells.   2s   6d

1620 **Aston Abbotts, Buckinghamshire**
(Farmiloe and Nixseaman)
For leatherings for the morris bells.   2d

1623 **Bray, Berkshire**   (Kerry)
Item, four coats for morris dancers, and
for the Maid Marian, and a pair of breeches
and doublet for the fool, and a cup.

1629 **Great Marlow, Buckinghamshire**   (Langley)
The morris coats were accounted for up till 1629.

* * * * *

One obvious conclusion that springs out of these accounts is that morris dancers were fed and clothed at the parish expense. This presumably means that morris provided an attraction that increased church takings by an amount at least equal to the expenditure. If this is true, and the church had some small dependence upon income from the morris, then we can understand how this gave a particularly painful twist to the tails of Puritans, and why they reserved a particular venom for events at the church/morris interface.

If we discount the expendable food and drink, then the other regularly mentioned articles are coats, bells and shoes. These, we may assume, made up the material equipment needed to turn a villager into a morris dancer. As time goes by it becomes clear that coats and bells were often church property, stored in the church and occasionally hired out to nearby parishes. Bells were mounted on leather garters and worn, so we can suppose, just below the knee in a manner very like modern Cotswold bell-pads. Coats were the most distinctive part of the kit and money was spent on buying cloth and then for the making, painting and, later on, for the washing of these coats. The fabric was commonly fustian, and if we look at the dress styles of those days we can guess that 'coat' meant a front-fastening jerkin that was belted-in at the waist and reached down to just above the knee. The decorative materials mentioned in the accounts, orseden, silver paper, gold skins and spangles, were presumably applied to the coat in some way or other, along with the paint. Washing such a coat must have been quite an undertaking.

The dozen direct mentions in this chapter which make it clear when, during the year, the dancing took place, show no agreement on a particular date or festival that might be regarded as a centre-point for the morris year. There are three mentions for Corpus Christi, two for Fair Day, two for Whitsun and one mention each for Dedication Day, Relic Sunday, May Day, the Sunday after May Day, and Midsummer Eve. The morris of the churchwardens' accounts came out to dance when the church arranged a suitable occasion, with little regard for what that occasion might be. This does not, of course, preclude the possibility of morris dancers having an unrecorded life outside the church circuit, but the fact that the church had to provide them with kit makes it look unlikely.

I have already made it clear that I disagree with the *Oxford Dictionary*'s claim that morris dancers usually dressed up as characters out of the Robin Hood legend.[1] On the other hand there is no doubt that the Robin Hood legend was a strong influence on some church gatherings of the early 1500s, when morris dancers were beginning to appear in public for the first time. If we insist upon standing on firm evidence, then there is not a lot more we can say about the Robin Hood/morris relationship – but there are still some ideas that shine like will-o'-the-wisps, tempting us onto less stable ground. This is, perhaps, a suitable place to dabble with temptation and venture out to see what these ideas have to offer.

At centre stage stands, not Robin Hood himself, but Maid Marian – and the Concordance (following Chapter 4) has already introduced us to some of the complexities and confusions that lie within this name. Robin Hood did not always have a Maid Marian: indeed, for the whole of the fifteenth century Robin managed to hold down his job as folk hero without female company. Then, round about 1500, Robin picked up this girl. Where did she come from? Nobody seems to be very sure, but a favoured theory tells of a Marian in the romantic pastoral literature of France. And where did morris come from? That's a question that requires a full reading of this book, but fifty years before 1500 there was an entertainment popular in the courts of northern France that we have called ring morris – and ring morris had a lady in the middle. Moving into England, the very first churchwarden account to mention morris (Kingston, 1507/8) also records payment of 8d "For a gown for the lady". Putting these elements together we can work them into a story that goes something like this.

Once upon a time of comparative peace toward the end of Henry VII's reign, when the Wars of the Roses had been finally resolved by a bit of murder and a useful marriage, we can imagine a cheerful spirit of hope running through the villages, helped along as returning soldiers put the energy of youth back into a round of agricultural labour. We can also see, perhaps, a growth in village population with longer life-spans and a kindlier

---

[1] For a statement published in 1989 it is manifestly absurd.

attitude toward the sick; this would have put an increasing burden on parish funds. Certainly the church found a need to increase its income, and the occasional Church Ale was turned into a regular programme of fund-raising Games. Just as a Lord of Misrule was employed to organise entertainment in the big houses, so a young man was appointed to lead these parish Games. With one eye on the next war, the authorities looked with favour upon young men who spent time at weapons training, so it is therefore not surprising when this Games Leader took upon himself the name of that popular and traditional hero and arch-exponent of skill-at-arms – Robin Hood.

Robin noticed the arrival of a troupe of entertainers, performing dances that had been popular many years ago when the soldiers were over in France. With these dancers came an elegantly dressed young woman – there, because tradition dictated that she should be – nobody could quite remember why. So she just stood around looking pretty and serving as an audience. Robin immediately recognised that this girl had potential: the job she was doing for the dancers could very usefully be expanded to cover the whole of his Game, and so he adopted the idea, giving his girl a name that combined something of the Church's reverence for the Virgin Mary, something out of a romantic French past, and something from a peasant memory of a rather more earthy wood-sprite. The newly-named Maid Marian then set out to create an important role in a long-established line that had started with the Summer Queens and continued on to give us May Queens, Carnival Queens and, ultimately, Miss World (where a whisper of the untouchable virgin still lingers on in the obligatory title 'Miss'). Marian took up a place in the Robin Hood stories: first as a pure and unspotted companion for Robin; later, as a very spotted friend of Friar Tuck.

It needs to be said in capital letters, THE LAST THREE PARAGRAPHS ARE SPECULATION: BELIEF IS OPTIONAL.

There is no real explanation for the appearance of morris at village Games, and the only justification for my story is a conviction that something known as morisque in France was likely to have some connection with something called morris in England. If true, the story helps us to cross a difficult gap in the evidence by giving a good strong link to connect together ladies with rings, ladies in gowns and Maids Marian. Put rather more plainly, it shows how the ring morris that we have seen presented in the closed environment of an aristocratic court in northern Europe could possibly have emerged and changed into the sort of morris we know, performed on an English village green, open to anyone who cares to stop and watch. This is a step that is vital to anyone wishing to see Kingston, 1507, as a link in a chain, rather than an original creation: it is also a step made shaky, because we have no idea what the Kingston morris dancers were actually doing.

If you didn't like that story – try this one. A curious and peculiarly English element of tradition takes a man who lived by robbery and violence; gives him a certain style; emphasises his bravery, and he becomes an object for admiration – even a hero. His crimes then fade to become little more than amusing pranks. In the world of fiction this is fine, but there is much evidence for this same attitude spreading into the real world, from Hereward the Wake in the aftermath of William's conquest, onward to the highwaymen of the eighteenth century. Robin Hood is certainly the best-known name in this long tradition and his tales were popular from late in the fourteenth century and all the way through the fifteenth. So, when the church needed to increase funds, who better to run the show than a popular hero who already had a reputation for gathering money? Perhaps it was at this point that a new thread was woven into the story – that Robin took from the rich, only to give to the poor. (He was now working for the church!) It is not therefore surprising that one of the festivals at Kingston was called 'The Robin Hood Game', with a leader/organiser/performer called Robin Hood. Morris dancers made their first public performances at Kingston. Did Robin Hood and the dancers coalesce? I don't think so. I have danced for the Townswomen's Guild but I didn't become a townswoman. Yes, the morris dancers included in their group a lady, but there is absolutely no evidence for what she did: most likely she was a descendant of the lady with the ring. Did this lady transmogrify into Maid Marian? Again, I don't think so. I prefer to see the morris dancers, together with their lady, being booked as part of the entertainment at a fundraising church show led by someone taking the name Robin Hood who sometimes had an assistant called Maid Marian. That, and nothing more.

CHAPTER 7: ACCOUNT BOOK ENTRIES FROM
ENGLISH PARISH CHURCHES
Summary

HFA numbers refer to Heaney, Forrest, *Annals of Early Morris*

		HFA			HFA
1507/8	Kingston	14	1558	Leicester	105
1509/10	Kingston	22	1560	Abingdon	112
1513	Reading	29	1562	West Tarring	115
1515/16	Kingston	32	1562/63	Southampton	117
1519/20	Kingston	37	1563	Northill	119
1521/22	Kingston	46	1565	Northill	127
1527	Dunmow	B11	1571	London	145
1529	Reading	61	c.1575	Dunmow	149
1530	Reading	66	1585	St Columb Major	A20
1530	Guildford	65	1591	London	237
1532	Dunmow		1595	Great Marlow	260
1536/37	Kingston	73	1602	Bray	326
1537/38	Kingston	77	1603	Leicester	337
1540	Maldon	79	1608	Great Marlow	
1541/42	Reading	80	1612	Great Marlow	393
1553	Reading	94	1620	Aston Abbotts	446
1554	Abingdon		1623	Bray	470
1557	Reading	102	1629	Great Marlow	495

There are thus:-
7 entries from Kingston-upon-Thames, Surrey;
6 from Reading, Berkshire;
4 from Great Marlow, Buckinghamshire;
3 from Dunmow, Essex;
2 from Abingdon, Oxfordshire;
       Bray, Berkshire
       Leicester;
       London;
       Northill, Bedfordshire
and single entries from Aston Abbotts, Buckinghamshire;
       Guildford, Surrey;
       Maldon, Essex;
       St Columb Major, Cornwall;
       Southampton, Hampshire;
       Tarring, Sussex.

CHAPTER 8

SOME ILLUSTRATIONS OF MORISCO

The very earliest illustrations of what might be called morisco come from one of the great books in the Bodleian Library: a gloriously illuminated manuscript, Bodley 264, *The Romance of Alexander*. Some description of this book has already been given in Chapter 6 under the date 1344 (page 96). There are four pages that show us dancing figures and two pages where people wear animal heads in the manner of a disguising, as discussed in Chapter 5.

1a. Folio 84V This is the one used by Strutt. Five men in line hold hands and dance to the sound of bagpipe and portative organ. They wear a one-piece hood and cape, where the sides of the hood are extended to a point with a bell. The midriff appears bare and they wear coloured hose with what I can only describe as a nappy. (Technical books on costume refer to these garments as braies.)

Illustration 1a
Detail from the bottom of a page in *The Romance of Alexander* of 1344.
Bodleian Library, Oxford.

Illustration 1b
Detail from the bottom of a page in *The Romance of Alexander* of 1344.
Bodleian Library, Oxford.

1b. Folio 78R Five men in line hold hands and dance (could it be a hey?). They each wear a pixie hood and a smock.

1c. Folio 51V Five men in line, this time each joined to his neighbour by holding the end of a short cord each and they dance vigorously. They wear a pixie hood and a smock.

Illustration 1d
Detail from the bottom of a page in *The Romance of Alexander* of 1344.
Bodleian Library, Oxford.

1d. Folio 129R Five men in line hold hands and may be dancing a hey: number five carries a handbell. They wear coloured smocks and a hood with a long tubular extension at the back that was known as a liripipe. A musician plays a large tambourine while, rather strangely, two men carry a third away on a stretcher. Could this be the very first morris injury?

152

1e. Folio 181V This is another illustration used by Strutt. Five men stand in line holding hands and wearing splendid golden capes. They each have an animal's head: ass, monkey, ram, ox and gryphon. They wear colourful smocks and each has a dagger in his belt (see page 79).

Illustration 1f
Full page from *The Romance of Alexander*.
Find it on the Internet and see the amazing colours!

1f Folio 21V At the foot of a page of absolutely astonishing artwork we see a man with a lute, and five figures in line holding hands, three men and two women. The men wear heads of a stag, a rabbit and one of the mythical menagerie.

If we call this group of drawings from the Alexander Romance 'number one' on our list of illustrations, then 'number two' is the one usually given the reference title *Liber Particularis*, and this has been described in Chapter 6 under the date 1438 (page 100). 'Number three', at 1458, comprises the three silver cups of Alice Wetenhale engraved with morris dancers. These cups no longer exist so, although we can say with certainty that they illustrated morris dancers, we have no idea what they looked like. Thus the *Alexander* and the *Liber Particularis* give us picture but no title, whereas Wetenhale confirms the title but gives us no picture.

The *Liber Particularis* is Illustration 2 and the text of the Wetenhale Will is illustrated on page 104.

Illustration 2
Detail from a manuscript made in Padua in 1438, now in Wroclaw, Poland.
Usually referred to as *Liber Particularis*.

By a trick of history these oldest illustrations have come down to us with good, comfortable and secure dates, but from here onwards the path becomes rather more difficult: we need to consider the strange and sometimes outlandish illustrations that have been gathered together under the heading of 'Morisco' or, more recently, 'Ring Morris'. I have already given voice to some of my own reservations under the 1438 heading in Chapter 6, but we have to press on and look at these illustrations, most of which come to us out of a print collector's drawer as a single sheet without any clue as to either title or date.

I should, perhaps, start by making no claim to be an art historian, but I have looked long and hard at these pictures over many years and I am quite sure that, in spite of the cartoonist treatment, they all share a recognisably similar 'sense of occasion' which convinces me that they started off with real, live performances. Concerning the dates, various opinions have been offered for individual pictures, but I have come to the conclusion that all of them can be parcelled up together into a thirty-year time-span (from 1480 to 1510) with very little left hanging out at the ends. Having tidied up their dates, I shall call this group 'The Renaissance Collection'.

The Renaissance Collection

All in this group are attributable to the period 1480–1510 and are therefore presented here in no particular order. The heading for each item is intended to serve only as a convenient label for reference purposes and should not be taken as a hint of deeper meaning.

4. Van Meckenem Circular

An engraving by Israel Van Meckenem in the British Museum fills a circular space and shows three dancers cavorting around a stylishly dressed lady with a ring, in company with a musician playing pipe and tabor and a fool with a bauble. They dance in a small, simple room with an audience looking in through the window. The bauble, incidentally, is usually a staff with a fool's head carved on one end.

Illustration 4
The circular engraving by Israel Van Meckenem. British Museum.

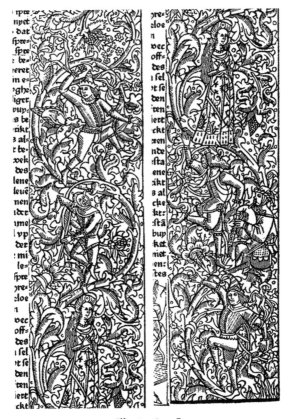

Illustration 5
A single vertical strip (here cut in order to fit) from the Cologne Bible
of about 1480 in the British Library.

5. Cologne Bible

Early printed books often filled in empty spaces with any woodcut that the printer happened to have lying around. Alongside the introductory remarks in a bible printed about 1480, there is a column of figures entwined in greenery. There are three dancers with bells at elbow, wrist, knee and ankle; a lady with a ring; a musician playing bagpipe and a fool with a staff. (British Library)

6. *'La promenade et la danse'*

This title appears under the picture, but looks like a later addition. The Warburg Institute has a photograph of what Lowe describes as an engraving on ivory: it shows two dancers circling a lady with a ring; a musician with a pipe (and possibly a tabor) and a fool with bauble; a man, three women and a girl look on. They all stand on paving in front of a screen of twining greenery.

Illustration 6
'La Promenade et la Danse'

Illustration 7
Called 'The Florentine Chessboard' but probably made in Burgundy.

7. Florentine chessboard

An ivory carving on the edge of a chessboard shows five dancers (four with ankle bells), three of whom have large curved swords of the 'stage Turk' variety. A lady, a musician playing pipe and tabor and a fool with bauble perform in a line among greenery. (Photo in the Warburg Institute)

8. Roundel

A photograph in the Warburg Institute shows a roundel, three and a half inches in diameter, probably of carved ivory. It shows two dancers, a lady

157

with a ring, a pipe and taborer and a fool with bauble. They seem to perform behind a gate in a fence.

Illustration 8
A small carved ivory roundel of Burgundian origin, in the British Museum.

9. 'Chorea Mundi'

Here we have an engraving with a title (Dance of the World) in three languages, and a signature of the artist (Joan Baptista Vrints). Put simply, there are six dancers around a lady with a musician and a fool, but the impact lies in the detail. The musician has a fiddle in his pocket but plays a woodwind instrument draped with sausages. The lady, in royal dress, holds a crystal ball and has an orb on her head. The fool emerges from under the lady's gown holding a face-mask and a jew's harp. The dancers have bells, sometimes on wrists, sometimes on ankles, and, in the case of the dancer with a hoop who is standing on his head, a baldric of bells. One dancer carries a flaming torch, another has the fool's bauble and a third balances a cup on his head. A crown and sheaf are marked *'Vanitas'*, which may give us some clue as to the artist's intention. (Douce prints in the Bodleian Library)

Illustration 9
The *'Chorea Mundi'* by Joan Baptista Vrints, from the
Douce collection in the Bodleian Library.

Illustration 10
'Satyrical Morisco' is my suggestion for a title. (Possibly by Squarcione,
who died 1468. Perhaps my dating of 1480–1510 was a bit tight.)

10. Satyrical Morisco

Nine heavily built individuals have faces that I am sure would have been recognised by the intended viewers (polititians, perhaps?). Six dancers have bells at wrist and ankle. The 'lady' holds up a cloven hoof and has a pointed staff over her shoulder on which are spiked eight loaves of bread (well, that's my guess). Two musicians play horns. A signature 'S.E.' is laterally reversed. (Warburg Institute)

11. A second, very similar but not identical etching is reproduced in Forrest's *History of Morris Dancing*. This one is marked 'D.H.' (Daniel Hopfer).

Illustration 12
A carved comb from Burgundy, in the Victoria and Albert Museum.

12. Carved comb

A photograph of a carved ivory comb in the Warburg Institute shows two dancers, a lady, a pipe and taborer and a fool with bauble. (The other side shows a stag hunt.)

Illustration 13
Ivory casket lid.
Noted by the Victoria and Albert Museum as Flemish or North Italian.

13. Ivory casket

Another photograph in the Warburg Institute shows a carved panel from a casket in the Victoria and Albert Museum which has six figures individually framed: three dancers, a lady with an apple, a pipe and taborer and a fool with bauble.

14. A second ivory casket panel in very similar style also has three dancers, but in rather more energetic pose, together with a lady, a pipe and taborer and a fool with a curiously bent bauble.

Illustration 15
'Florentine nude morris.' (My suggested title)

15. Florentine nude morris

The strangest print among the Warburg Collection shows nine male dancers, naked save for wrist bells and a headband with plume, one of whom stands on his hands, all circle round an equally naked lady with a ring and a small, but strategically placed, drape. Overhead a cherub plays pipe and tabor.

16. *Goldenes Dachl*

Under the Golden Roof at Innsbruck there is a frieze by the famous wood carver Erasmus Grassser which shows seven dancers, a lady with ring, a pipe and taborer and a fool (Lowe). There is here a backward bend of the torso that looks more like contortionist than dancer.

17. Munich woodcarvings

The Munich City Museum houses a superb set of ten carved wooden figures, each a bit over two feet tall, and their English label reads 'Erasmus Grasser's Morris Dancers'. By amazing good fortune an account book

162

survives recording a payment of 150 pounds 4 shillings to master Erasmus on 14 August 1480 for sixteen '*maruschka tanntz*' figures. These figures were made to embellish the hall of the Munich Rathaus, and the six pieces that are now missing are thought to have included the lady, the musician and the fool. It should be said that these statues stand (or should it be dance) among the world's great works of art. Each one is different: different clothes, different posture, different gestures and the faces suggest very different individuals. Three are illustrated here.

Illustration 17
Three of the ten surviving carved wooden figures of morris dancers in the Munich City Museum, 1480.

18. Flemish miniature

A photograph in the Warburg Institute of an item in the Brussels Royal Library has the quality of a quick sketch with a vaguely 'art nouveau' look. Three dancers (with probably a fourth coming in through the door) wear grass skirts and have bells at the waist and knee. One seems to hold a plate of soup behind his back – can it be an early custard pie? The lady is dressed for the harem with bare feet, loose trousers and a turban. The fool passes his bauble under his leg. A large audience sporting dramatic headgear watch from behind a barrier.

Illustration 18
The 'Flemish miniature' – another work that probably started life in Burgundy.

19. Woodcut marked 'HL'

There is a print by Hans Leinberger in the Warburg collection. A heap of people at the centre are either celebrating or brawling: arms and legs protrude from the heap but it is not possible to assess their number or function. Around the heap four men dance wildly and the lady holds an apple and possibly a hat. A pipe and taborer plays, and the fool has a double-headed bauble. From a cushioned gallery king, queen and courtiers watch, attended by their own fool. A large turnip occupies a significant space in the foreground.

Illustration 19
Woodcut by Hans Leinberger.

20. *Orchesography* cover

The Dover Publications' 1967 edition of Arbeau's *Orchesography* shows on its cover the central figures taken from an engraving by Hans Burgkmair (or possibly Albrecht Dürer) in the British Library. Six dancers, three men and three women, hold hands and dance sedately in a circle. It is quite unlike the other illustrations in this Renaissance Collection and the only reason for including it here is blackface: the men either have their faces painted black, or have black nets covering their faces (it is difficult to tell the intention on an engraving). This could lead to them being described as 'morisco dancers'. Courtiers watch from a gallery.

Illustration 21
The rectangular engraving by Israel Van Meckenem. British Museum.

21. Van Meckenem rectangular

I round off this Renaissance Collection as I started it, with Israel Van Meckenem. The reason for leaving this one till last is the much-talked-about relationship it has with the Betley window of (probably) 1621 (see Chapter 2 under 1778). This Van Meckenem engraving in the British Museum is of a rectangular panel of twining greenery inhabited by six dancers, a lady with apple, a musician with pipe and tabor, a fool with bauble, and a dog with a stick. So what of the similarities with Betley? If we count the illustrated panels of the Betley window starting top left and finishing with number twelve, the friar: then panels 2, 3, 6, 9 and 10 have strong similarities with the poses of dancers in the Van Meckenem engraving, but in each case laterally reversed. Although the poses match, it is debatable whether there is much similarity in the clothing. Two slight problems remain, however. The cropped edges of the Betley panels hint that the window may have been installed elsewhere before being built into the 1621 house (thus upsetting the date); and the lateral reversing could suggest that the engraving was copied from the window, which would confuse all our ideas. The most probable solution is that both were copied from a third picture, now lost, which showed only four dancers and a right-handed musician.

* * * * *

Anyone wishing to cast the net wider could, of course, include the *Liber Particularis* in this Renaissance Collection, and also, if they so wished, those items that have title but no picture (for without a picture none can contradict): Wetenhale, 1458; Chaworth, 1458; the Burgundy salts, 1467; Jackson, 1510; and Henry VIII's salt, inventoried 1532 but clearly made earlier.

So how can we summarise this Renaissance Collection? Seventeen illustrations lead me to believe that real performances took place with a handful of dancers, a lady and a fool, with a musician almost invariably playing pipe and tabor. The performance was a display in front of an audience, and an audience of royal, or near royal status. Bells I take to be optional extras, not absolutely essential to the dance, and for those who still have Cotswold morris at the back of their minds, similarity of either clothing or movement between the dancers was not required. And where did these performances take place? If you drew a line from Bruges to Florence and then marked all the great houses within a dozen miles of this line, I think you would have a rough idea, but court fashions spread far and fast.

A final reminder – not one of these pictures has an early label saying 'morris' or 'morisco' (apart from the Munich figures, where the translation of *'maruschka tanntz'* into 'morris dance' seems to be fairly sound, but here, sadly, three of the essential characters have gone missing). We know that the term 'morris dance' was in use at the time in England (see Wetenhale and the accounts of Henry VII), while 'morisco', or an obviously related word, was used on the Continent. Was morris dance the same as morisco? I think we have to say 'yes', or at least, that both were variants of the same thing. Was the ring morris of the Renaissance Collection the same as morisco and morris dance? Again I think we have to say 'yes', because to say 'no' would be to postulate a time when a dance without a name coexisted with a name without a dance.

* * * * *

22. c. 1490 – York Minster

In *English Dance and Song* of July/August 1987 Philip Underwood drew our attention to a single figure in a stained glass window in the Zouche chapel of York Minster. This figure plays pipe and tabor and appears to have bells at knee, belt, wrist and the hem of his tunic. From his appearance he would fit very easily with some of the groups in the Renaissance Collection. Indeed, if he had had suitable companions then he would have been included in that Collection as the only English representative.

23. c. 1520 – Beverley Minster

A misericord in Beverley Minster shows five figures, four of whom wear fool's caps. One plays pipe and tabor, another has a bladder on a stick and the others seem to be dancing. Should they be in this book at all? I'm not sure.

24. c. 1525 – Lancaster Castle

A carved oak panel about two feet long was removed from Lancaster Castle at some unknown date and is now kept in the Lancaster City Council Museum. The dating is extremely uncertain and the date given above is no more than my best guess: it could be thirty, or even forty years either way. There are four dancers, a woman with a ladle, a pipe and taborer and a fool with a bauble. The fool does look very similar to the one on the Betley window (although laterally reversed) and the dancers can all be matched for posture (reversed) on Betley, although the costumes are different. As mentioned when discussing the Van Meckenem Rectangular, I think we may be hinting at a lost original, parent to all three.

Illustration 24
The panel from Lancaster Castle, now in Lancaster City Museum.

Two of the figures require our more detailed attention. First the woman (and in this case I think 'woman' is a more appropriate term than 'lady'): she looks like a working member of the group carrying a pot or ladle, perhaps to solicit coins from an audience – very different from the lady whose only function was to stand in the middle and look pretty. If the purpose was indeed to collect money, then we are seeing a major social change: no longer were they a group booked by a lord to entertain his guests – they were out to entertain the general public and fund their activities by public generosity, a big step towards the present day. In Cecil Sharp's time any picture of a woman in a morris context had to be a man in woman's clothing: in this case I think he might just be right. The skirt, in particular, is very odd. Books of costume cannot show me that skirt length in any of the likely centuries. Could it be a man's jacket with the part below the waist extended? Or, more likely, could it be the wife's dress with half a metre chopped off the bottom?

The other curious figure is third from the left: the first dancer. Here there are problems with the Cecil Sharp rule – how does a boy in woman's clothing get away with being nude? Anne Gilchrist (1933) refers to "A nude girl dancer (or a curly-headed boy personating a girl, with the aid of artificial feminine characteristics)", I notice he also wears a loin cloth, which must help. Some have noted the curly hair and the rather broad features and suggested that she or he was a negro, leading to a fairly fruitless discussion of moor, morien, marian and morris. Nudity itself should not come to us as any great surprise: we have just noted the 'Florentine nude morris' and in Chapter 6 the Midsummer Watch Procession of 1521 had 60 moryans, naked boys dyed black (and also a woman morian). And who could forget Fetherston's condemnation of morris dancers who danced naked in nets!

This Lancaster panel might be very important, but it is plagued with uncertainties. Was it carved in England, showing things that went on in England? Or was it brought home as a souvenir of a holiday in Belgium? It obviously belongs to the same family as the Renaissance Collection and, if it is English, then it is the only English member of that Collection. But it does seem to have moved on a bit if the idea of collecting money from an audience is correct. In the 1525 entry in Chapter 6 we seem to see morris dancers becoming an independent group, and this might be relevant.

Try this for a thumbnail sketch. Ring morris, or morisco, was a tremendously popular entertainment in the great houses of mainland Europe. However, it did not reach England until the whole idea was running out of steam and a new idea of a popular morris was taking hold. The Lancaster panel illustrates this point of changeover (possibly).

25. 1600 – Kemp's jig

It is with some sense of relief that we arrive at 1600 and meet, for the first time, an illustration that is free of doubts. We know it was drawn to represent a morris dancer and we know it was drawn in 1600 (see Chapter 2). With a feather in his hat, his floral shirt, his open sleeves blowing in the wind and with bell-pads in the Cotswold manner, Will Kemp dances on towards Norwich to the tunes of his pipe and taborer, Tom Slye. See illustration on p. 17.

Should anyone doubt these long open sleeves on Will Kemp and on two of the Betley window dancers, Tollet quotes from Markham's *Art of Angling*, 1635, which requires a fisherman's clothing to be "without hanging sleeves, waving loose, like sails".

Illustration 26
Cruikshank's copy of 'a picture painted in a sort of stone colour, shaded with brown'.

26. Early 1600s? – 'Fools' Morris Dance'

In Hone's *Ancient Mysteries* (1823) there is an etching by Mr Cruikshank copying "a picture painted in a sort of stone colour, shaded with brown". It seems to show a performance on a stage, and so I would be inclined to date the original painting to the first quarter of the seventeenth century when stage morris was popular (see Chapter 6) – but is this a picture of morris? As I read the scene, five fools are having their performance interrupted by a stilt-walker from a rival group. The fools wear hats like a night-cap, coats cut to points at the hem and a generous set of bells at the shin. Two musicians play: one flute and one drum. Hone gave them the title "Fools' Morris Dance" and there is little doubt that they are a group of stage fools, but the claim to be morris dancers would seem to hang on the bells alone. However, one important point should not escape our notice: William Hone probably knew as much, if not more, about morris dancing as anyone else in his day – and he thought they were morris.

Illustration 27
A drawing of the dancers that appear on a whalebone book cover found in Co. Dublin.

27. Early 1600s? – Munster bone plate

Also attributed to the first quarter of the seventeenth century is a scene of five dancers that appears at the foot of a bone plate engraved with heraldic devices (in the National Museum, Dublin). Both the figures themselves, and the way they are presented on the page, show an uncanny resemblance to the Alexander Romance of 1344, although it is almost impossible to imagine how any connection could have been made. Joseph Needham included a tracing of these figures in his 'Geographical Distribution of English Ceremonial Dance Traditions' (*JEFDSS*, 1936). One dancer carries a sword and two dancers have a tambourine, or it may be a hat. Three of the dancers are linked together by holding the ends of a short cord or, as Needham fancifully suggests, a rapper sword.[1] The original is not very clear, so a tracing is substituted.

---

[1] Recent information (2005) from the National Museum of Ireland corrects and expands these notes. The object is a whalebone book cover found in the parish of Donabate, near Swords, Co. Dublin. The heraldic devices are the coat of arms of the Fitzgerald Earls of Desmond and the museum places the object in the sixteenth century.

28. c. 1620 – Vinckenboom painting

A painting in the Fitzwilliam Museum, Cambridge, called *The Thames at Richmond* shows the old Richmond Palace across the river, while in the foreground a small group dance for their audience. This group has been the subject of much comment over many years, but everybody has accepted that they are morris dancers. Captain Grose traced five of the figures and an engraving was prepared (laterally reversed and with the positions slightly adjusted) and published 1 January 1808 (in Douce). The painting also makes the cover shot on John Forrest's *History* (1999).

Illustration 28
Part of a painting called *The Thames at Richmond* in the Fitzwilliam Museum at Cambridge. Once thought to be by Vinckenboom, it is now described as 'Flemish School'.

This scene shows a number of new features that deserve our attention. First, and perhaps the most important, the dancers are performing in a public space and covering their costs by making a collection from passers-by. There was a suggestion of this in the Lancaster Castle panel, but here at Richmond it is quite clear. The audience is also worth a closer look: they are, I would suggest, a gentry couple with their daughter; a merchant couple giving money; a village couple; a woman on a packhorse and (well known to every morris dancer) a stray dog. The hint is probably intentional – morris appeals to all classes. The shape of the dance is one we have not seen before, four dancers on a single line: although anybody who has seen a performance of the dance Cecil Sharp collected from Brimfield in Herefordshire on Boxing Day 1909 will recognise this shape immediately.

The performers comprise four dancers, one of whom is, or is dressed as, a woman; a musician with pipe and tabor; a fool in a coat cut to points at shoulder and hem; and a man with a hobby horse hung round his hips. The fool is an ancient character and here he carries what is often called a ladle, although I think a wooden spoon would be a better description. I assume the purpose of the spoon is to increase the distance between a smelly fool and his slightly less smelly donor. To the inboard end of the spoon is attached a bladder.

Hobby horses had been around for a long time as floating characters, joining in processions, celebrations, and more recently, in the theatrical shows. Here in Richmond, I think the morris dancers saw a need for an extrovert link between the dancers and the audience in addition to the fool, now that collecting money was important. It just so happened that the hobby horse was handy.

Douce tells us who the lady is, and is rather unnecessarily rude: "Maid Marian is not remarkable for the elegance of her person". Three dancers and the hobby horse have beards: Maid Marian does not – I think she is a woman.

Finally, and I make this point rather quietly, are we looking at a painting worked up from sketches of an actual event, or are we seeing a commissioned painting of a palace which has, by way of foreground interest, a collection of figures that the artist thought might be appropriate for a riverside event?

(The latest opinion is that this painting is not by Vinckenboom and should be described as 'Flemish School'. However, the Vinckenboom label is so well known that I shall continue to use it even if it is not technically accurate.)

29. 1621 – The Betley window

We have already considered Mr Tollet's *Opinion concerning the Morris Dancers upon his Window* in Chapter 2, and also mentioned possible linkages with the Van Meckenem rectangular engraving and with the Lancaster Castle panel, earlier in this chapter. We might also remind ourselves that the present opinion of the Victoria and Albert Museum places the date of the Betley costumes within the bracket 1490 to 1520, which ties in very nicely for an emergence from the Renaissance Collection and out into the public morris of may games. But again there is a slight niggling worry – the similarities we have noted between Van Meckenem, Lancaster and Betley have been based on posture and not on costume. To show the extent of these similarities it is worth making a list of the Betley panels (more correctly called 'quarries') starting from the top left and marking 'M' for similarities to Van Meckenem and 'L' to Lancaster.

1	Fool		L
2	Dancer	M	L
3	Dancer	M	L
4	Dancer		L
5	Maypole		
6	Musician	M	
7	Dancer		
8	Hobby horse		
9	Dancer	M	
10	Dancer	M	L
11	Lady		
12	Friar		

Thus we have six dancers (with bells at knee or ankle), a lady, a fool and a musician, who all fit well enough into the pattern we have seen in previous groups. The maypole is probably no more than the glass-painter's idea of an appropriate season and the friar might well have been brought in from the tales of Robin Hood. This leaves us with the hobby horse, which is so splendidly presented that Tollet suggested that it might be the King of May. The horse has in its mouth what is said to be a ladle for collecting money: this suggestion was presumably made by someone familiar with the Vinckenboom painting. Various explanations have been offered for what appear to be two daggers pointed at (or penetrating) the 'rider's' cheeks. None seems satisfactory. I think we probably have a graphic illustration of a story now forgotten, just as we keep coming across the words "For lo, the hobby horse is forgot" – clearly the punch line for a joke that was so well known it did not need to be recorded.

Illustration 29
The famous 'Betley Window' in the Victoria and Albert Museum.

30. 1633 – Perth glovers' costume

A costume is on display in the Perth Museum and Art Gallery. Refer to Chapter 6. I am not sure that the present author would have arranged the exhibit in quite this way.

Illustration 30
The Perth Glovers' sword dance dress (1633) as displayed in the Perth Museum and
Art Gallery.

Illustration 31
A sculptured stone sign once marking the 'Three Morris Dancers' pub in London.

31. c. 1648 – 'Three Morris Dancers' pub sign

Printed illustrations survive of a sculptured stone sign that is now lost. See Chapter 6. There are three dancers, two men and one woman. The men wear a long and loose night-shirt type of garment belted up at the waist to give a calf-length hemline, and they wear a hood drawn upwards to a point which bends over, with a bell(?) at the point. The woman wears a tightly fitted bodice and a full skirt at ankle length. A man and the woman hold unidentifiable objects.

32. 1650 – Woodcut

A work called *Recreation for ingenious head-peeces*, printed in 1650, included a woodcut of a single morris dancer with handkerchiefs and a crossed baldric. Underneath is a verse from 1646 that starts,

"With a noyse and a din
Comes the Maurice Dancer In"

The cut and the verse were published again by Dibdin, 1808, and by Burton, 1891.

Illustration 32
A woodcut printed in 1650.

Illustration 33
The only item in the British National Collection of Coins and Medals to show morris dancers. Token coin issued by John Lisle, probably in the later 1660s.

33. c. 1665 – 'Three Morris Dancers' token

The background to the issue of these trade tokens was described in Chapter 6, under 1648. The three dancers illustrated each has a single band of bells round his left ankle, two wear a pointed hat with a brim and the central figure has a large hat in the night-cap style. They appear to wear an all-over garment belted at the waist. (The figures are only eight millimetres high.)

Illustration 34
Small woodcut from Holme's *Academy of Armory*.

34. 1688 – *Academy of Armory*

This is a book by Randle Holme designed to assist anyone trying to construct a coat of arms, by providing them with information and sketches of a vast array of items that they might choose to include. A small woodcut shows two morris dancers in jacket and breeches with bells at knee and elbow. One has a pointed hat with two bells and the other a broad-brimmed hat with a feather, and each holds what looks like a handkerchief in his right hand.

35. c. 1725 – Dixton harvesters

A large painting in the Cheltenham Art Gallery and Museum was reproduced in the *Observer* Magazine of 4 November 1979. This picture shows a broad swathe of countryside near Dixton (five miles from Cheltenham) where all the locals are busy at haymaking, and in the bottom right corner a morris dance is in progress. For the very first time we see here a set of dancers that look closely similar to a present-day Cotswold side: they are all dressed the same; and they are all doing more or less the same thing. This element of uniformity and teamwork some modern dancers might see as the start of a real morris. They wear white shirts, black breeches, white socks and black shoes and each has a crossed baldric, three of them red and three blue: the hats could be tricorns. The six dancers stand in a single line waving a handkerchief in each hand, while at the head of the set three men wave long sticks with a bunch of ribbons at the end: one dressed in the manner of the dancers and two in dark clothing. There is no sign of a musician.

Illustration 35
A very small part of a very large painting in Cheltenham Art Gallery and Museum showing harvesters at Dixton.

36. c.1805 – Lichfield bower procession

A watercolour by C.E. Stringer, dated to somewhere between 1787 and 1823, was found slipped into a book in the Bodleian Library and is reproduced in Michael Heaney's booklet *Bedlam Morris*. It shows a musician with pipe and tabor, a man/woman and a fool with a bauble, being followed by eight dancers in shirt and breeches clashing sticks: there are no hats or bells. These are followed by two drummers and a party carrying guns. (See also Chapter 6, under 1798.)

37. 1818 – Stowe House

Keith Chandler's book *Ribbons, Bells and Squeaking Fiddles* has on its cover a painting of morris dancing at Stowe House in Buckinghamshire, the original of which is now in the County Museum, Aylesbury. There are two musicians, drum and flute, and six dancers in the usual Cotswold formation of three facing three. They wear shirt, breeches, a crossed baldric and a top hat with ribbons, and they clash sticks vigorously.

Illustration 36
A watercolour of the Lichfield bower procession by C.E. Stringer, in the Bodleian.

Illustration 37
A painting owned by the Buckinghamshire Archaeological Society shows morris dancers at Stowe House in 1818.

Illustration 38
Morris dancers and rushcart at the Failsworth Pole (near Manchester).

38. c. 1820 – Failsworth, near Manchester

A splendid engraving of the Failsworth rush-bearing, somewhere around 1820, is reproduced in Burton's *Rush-Bearing* of 1891. It shows the 'Failsworth Pole' (about 45 feet high) and the approaching rushcart drawn by three horses. Alongside there are six morris dancers in shirt, breeches and crossed baldric, some with top hats. Three of the dancers wave in their right hands something that might be a hank of yarn. They are led by two musicians, flute and drum, and a flag carrier.

39. 1821 – Manchester

A painting of a rushcart and morris dancers in Long Millgate, Manchester, by Roger Wilson, is also reproduced in Burton's *Rush-Bearing*. The rushcart seems to have come to a halt beside a rowdy crowd while the morris dancers perform in the background. The dancers are obviously wearing long trousers but the rest of the details are unclear: probably a baldric of some sort and perhaps a decorated hat. One banner among the crowd reads 'Peace', and on another the only word legible is 'Love'.

Illustration 39
A painting by Roger Wilson of morris dancers and rushcart in Long Millgate,
Manchester, 1821.

40. 1825 – Sketches sent to Hone's *Year Book*

Another entry in Burton's *Rush-Bearing* refers to a draft letter from Jesse Lee about the Lancashire Wakes, or Rush-Bearings. This letter included sketches of a rushcart and a detail of two young men pulling. The story usually told has the rushcart being drawn along by young men pulling on ropes, who danced as well as pulled. The few pictures we have show the rushcart drawn by horses, while the morris are dancing nearby. I know which I would rather do. Lee's sketch indicates two ropes from the sides of the rushcart with staves across in ladder fashion and the dancers pushing on these staves (while held head-high!). He suggests that forty to sixty men might be involved.

Illustration 40
A sketch included in a letter by Jesse Lee sent to Hone, 1825.

Illustration 41
George Scharf's sketch of dancers he saw in Green Street, Leicester Square, 1826.
British Museum

41. 1826 – London

George Scharf made a sketch of dancers he saw in Green Street, Leicester Square, and the sketch is reproduced in Keith Chandler's *Taking an Annual Circuit* (the original is in the British Museum). There are six dancers performing with sticks, plus a musician with pipe and tabor. There is an elegance of style and the dancers look more like curly-headed boys than farm labourers, so we are not quite sure what we are looking at. Are they sons of the well-to-do having a go? Are they a theatrical group practising in the street? Or did George Scharf simply smarten them up as he drew?

42. 1832 – Hone's *Year Book*

Hone published an engraving very loosely based on the sketches sent him by Jesse Lee. The rushcart is horse-drawn and in front six lads amble along carrying sticks: one of them shows signs of dancing.

Illustration 43
Copy from an old photograph of a painting of morris dancers at Lymm Cross,
Cheshire, about 1840.

43. 1840 – Lymm, Cheshire

A painting by an unknown artist, once lost but now in a storeroom at the Castle Museum at York, shows Lymm Cross with morris dancers and rushcart about 1840. The empty cart, drawn by four horses, is preceded by dancers in white shirts and trousers with baldric and waving handkerchiefs.

Although not very clear, the dancers seem to be in single file following a man in woman's clothing who brandishes what is usually referred to as a ladle. To my eye this utensil is not an appropriate shape for getting a helping of soup out of a pot, but it does look very similar to the bauble carried by fools some three hundred and fifty years earlier.

44. 1844 – Stowe House

A painting by James Danby (in private ownership) was reproduced on the cover of *English Dance and Song*, September/October 1957. The painting marked the occasion of the coming-of-age of the heir to the Duke of Buckingham in September 1844. It shows six dancers in the usual Cotswold formation (except that number three seems to have got lost): they wear low-crowned hats, white shirts and dark breeches with crossed baldrics and they are striking sticks (except number three). The owner of the painting added the information that the dancers are cross-gartered, some in blue, some in red, and that the baldrics were also some blue and some red. We should, perhaps, remind ourselves that these costumes were provided by the Duke and so there were influences at play other than pure tradition. The musician has a large drum and the fool wears a clown suit and a pointed hat and waves a bladder on a stick of quite unreasonable length. (See also Chapter 6 under this date.)

CHAPTER 8: SOME ILLUSTRATIONS OF MORISCO
Summary

CHAPTER 9

TOWARDS A CONCLUSION

At this point in the story we have completed a review of what might be called the positive evidence for morris dancing, and if you, the reader, are left feeling a bit confused then to some extent I have succeeded; for it is a confusing story and to present such a tale as simple and straightforward would have been dishonest. A number of the authors we met in Chapter 2 also admitted to being confused and they were well represented by Douce when he said, "Wherever we turn, nothing but irregularity presents itself". This confusion is, of course, a natural outcome of the patchy and inadequate state of the evidence, and much of Chapter 1 was devoted to a forewarning of this problem.

It is my intention to draw this book to a close with an attempt at a summary, but before I do so, there are one or two loose ends that need to be mentioned, even if they cannot be neatly tied together. It may help with a rather subtle point if we divide our thinking, for a moment, into two parts: the dance, morris; and the word, morris. There were pastimes that related to the word without necessarily being ancestor to the dance, and the first to come to mind is the Moor/Christian battle. Nothing I have seen or read of this battle leads me to connect it in any way with the movements and style of performance we see in English morris dancing. On the other hand, called Mourisca or Moreska, the battle clearly has a relationship with the word-link *morris – morisco – moorish* that is an inescapable part of how we came to call morris, morris. Thus we have something with a legitimate place in morris history that has absolutely nothing to do with the dance. If we accept this line of thought then the Moor/Christian battle gave nothing to morris apart from a name and we can stop trying to link morris onto a militaristic past. Since those other mock-fighting dances, Buffons and Matachins, attached themselves to the morris story only because they shared this military theme, then these too can be dropped. We now seem to have separated the English dance morris from any Spanish or Portuguese parentage.

What are we to make of the entertainments I have labelled 'Italian theatricals'? Often called moriscos, they were light-hearted interludes with a vaguely classical background, and here again there is a similarity of name, but probably not a similarity in performance. It may well be that this strand of Renaissance entertainment came over to England and joined onto the antic morris element that had been added into the masques. It also seems quite likely that this idea took on a rather more rustic tone and grew into the morris as seen on the public stage. Say 'morris' to a London theatregoer of the early seventeenth century and he or she would probably think of a hotchpotch display by stage clowns. A further strand from the Italian theatricals comes down to us as the *commedia dell'arte,* which is widely believed to be the source for both Punch and Judy and the Christmas pantomime.

I am aware that back in Chapter 1 I claimed that morris is what the ordinary people of the time referred to as 'morris', and this is still a useful starting point, although we can now see that there are some rather doubtful areas. One area that clearly does not fit is social dance. John Forrest quotes from a seventeenth-century manuscript in the British Library:

> *The Maurice daunce*
> "Lead all ye Mates round ye Roome.
> 1 ffig: The 1 & 2d Man meete the 1 & 2d woaman & passe
> through them to ye contrary sides & soe faces about then ye 1 & 2d
> Cu: take hands & meete each other then let goe hands & turne round
> all 4 single ——"

and so on.

Quite clearly this is the start of a fairly ordinary longways social dance, so why was it called morris? Perhaps it was a traditional-sounding word that might lend some authority to a currently fashionable dance. Perhaps the tune had something of a morris character. We don't know. There are a few other social dances that include morris in their title and perhaps the best known is Staines Morris, partly because of a good tune, and partly because a Longborough morris dance was set to the tune at a later date.

It is hardly necessary to point out the weaknesses in the morris story: they speak well enough for themselves. Were we right to follow Strutt and think of the five-men-in-line from 1344 as ancestors of the morris dance? Are these five-in-line related to those performers who come on, one after the other, in a moresque (as in 1468)? And what did the engravings on the Wetenhale cups really show? It is also uncomfortably true that the three strands that I have called proto-morris, the dance of five-in-line, the ring morris, and the Moor/Christian battle, are all predominantly based in continental Europe, with only the occasional reflection to be seen in England. We saw blackface linked to the name Moreskoes in Henry VIII's court, 1510, but was there ever a connection between blackface and the dance before the morris on the banks of the River Severn met up with the 'nigger minstrels' in the 1890s?

Then there are a whole range of other activities that appear from time to time running alongside morris: mummings and disguisings from the earliest times; sword dances that can so easily be linked to human sacrifice (always a great crowd-pleaser); and tournaments that drew competitors from one end of Europe to the other, circulating the latest ideas in fashion and fashionable pastimes, with the tournaments themselves providing a venue for any entertainer to make a bit of money. Then, at village level: the Feast of Fools; the Church Ales; Mayday; Maid Marian, sweeps and green men, and perhaps we can add in the idea of cross-dressing, which may have started out with some erotic potential but became humorous and was certainly another good way to wind up the clergy.

All these ideas share an element of uncertainty when we try to link them to morris dancing, simply through lack of clear evidence, and it is thus open to each one of us to make our own selection and build from this box of bricks an early history for morris to suit our own taste. Many have already done so, and strange have been some of the results. It is now time to come off the fence and select those elements that seem most secure and to set them out as a basic framework – a condensed history of the morris dance.

A Condensed History of the Morris Dance

We must start, I believe, with a vague and ill-defined activity found in the English countryside of the thirteenth and fourteenth centuries, usually referred to as a Summer Game. These Games might be looked upon as a sort of primaeval soup out of which emerged things like the King Game and the Mummers and that oldest tradition of all – antagonism from those in authority. One can imagine a Lord or Bishop being affronted by the very thought of serfs or peasants organising their own entertainment: they ought to be standing, cow-like, waiting to be told what to do by their betters!

Our next step has five men in line, holding hands or tied together, as in the *Romance of Alexander* or in the tragedy at Paris, 1392. Paris was a royal event, but Alexander suggests that this dance may have reached down to a more common level of society, and a hint by association links this dance to the mummers who wore animal heads (compare the entry for 1347). Strutt's influence leads us to call this five-man performance a 'Fool's Dance' and to see it as an ancestor of morris. The *Liber Particularis* illustration might be showing us an elaboration on this five-in-line theme with a lady and a fool added to the five dancers. It is also just possible that this dance took on something of a comic style and became ring morris of the sort that I have gathered up into the Renaissance Collection of 1480 to 1510.

Some sort of display dance called a 'morisque' (which might have been ring morris) became popular in the great houses of northern France, with records in 1440, 1457, 1458, 1459 (two) and 1468. Then overlapping with this French phase, we meet the first pieces of evidence for morris in England: the wills of Wetenhale and Chaworth in 1458; preparations at Lanhern in 1466; the Midsummer Watch procession of 1477, and onward into popularity at the English and Scottish courts in the first few years of the sixteenth century.

There is a vague impression about the early morris performances at court that the dancers were 'brought in' – from whence, we know not: perhaps it meant no more than being brought into the presence of the King. At first there seems to be a group of about six dancers who filled a spot in the evening's entertainment (although 1512 Scotland does show us a single dancer doing a solo). By 1511 we see the morris being made part of a pageant and by 1514 the whole performance, morris and all, is turning into a masque. In parallel with this court activity, the church at Kingston-upon-Thames brought morris to the general public for the very first time. The churchwardens recorded morris as an aid to church fundraising and morris went on to be used in this way for sixty years or so.

Great civic processions were held in London (see items from 1521 to 1559) and morris dancers took part. The merchant guilds were principal organisers and it may be that their overseas trading partners offered some suggestions for the style of morris performance. For it is here that we see, for the only time in England, some sort of a link with the continental 'mouriska' – the staged fight between Christians and dark-skinned Moors. Lords of Misrule and Mayday celebrations also became involved in these civic events. However, rising costs brought an end to the processions.

In 1571 an official church injunction required morris dancers (along with others who commit disorder) to be reported. From here on the churchwardens' accounts merely report possession of morris kit: there is not much evidence to suggest its use or its replacement, but on the other hand, there is no sign of it being deliberately destroyed. Puritan writings begin to colour the atmosphere, and country morris dancers find that the world is against them.

The Great Party at Kenilworth in 1575 was big enough to avoid the Puritan disapproval, but then it did present morris as being something from an ancient past.

Will Kemp, in 1600, is a major marker in our story and provides us with the first certain illustration of a morris dancer. The morris of civic processions had gone and the morris of village celebration, under the auspices of the church, had also disappeared. The only surviving morris was starting a new life on the popular stage, performed by professional actors. It was this stage morris that formed the background to Kemp's Nine Day's Wonder. This is, perhaps, a good place to remind ourselves of our ignorance concerning the dance: whether we are talking about civic processions, village celebrations or morris on the popular stage, we have absolutely no idea what dance movements were being used.

The fantastic tale of Old Meg of Herefordshire, 1609, must surely be the product of a fertile imagination, for it can have very little to do with the real world.

The *Book of Sports* of 1618 gave Royal Approval to a revival of village recreations including Whitsun Ales and morris dancing, much to the annoyance of the Puritan clergy. Putting two and two together (as a substitute for evidence) we could see Captain Dover's Olympic Games, recently started at Chipping Campden, providing the venue, and King James' Book providing the authority, for a start to morris in the Cotswolds. Something of this sort must have happened and we face again the unanswerable question, 'What sort of dance were they doing?' And did the idea come from a long strand of memory going back into the village past; or was it borrowed from the stage; or was it a completely new invention; or did it come from some combination of these? The Vinckenboom painting is perhaps our only possible clue.

The London pub sign of circa 1648, together with the related trade-tokens of the Three Morris Dancers, most probably took up the idea from popular stage performances.

In the fifty-six years following the Restoration there are a handful of references to morris dotted around the country, but there is not really enough of a common theme for us to draw any useful conclusions, until the Verney letters make it clear that rowdy Whitsun Ales were in full swing in Buckinghamshire in 1716 and that 'Morrises' were among them. The picture becomes even clearer with the Dixton painting of circa 1725 where, for the first time, we see a group of dancers that can easily be recognised as a Cotswold morris, and Keith Chandler tells us that by the 1730s at least eight Cotswold villages had active morris sides.

From the 1730s onward the nature of our evidence takes on a change of flavour. Rather than finding the chance survival that was characteristic of earlier records, we begin to feel the presence of researchers deliberately thumbing their way through the files of local newspapers in pursuit of morris. It was generally believed, from the last years of the nineteenth century onward, that the best morris came from the Cotswolds, and naturally both field and library research have been angled in this direction. Now it is almost certainly true that the Whitsun ales and fairs of the

Cotswold area did indeed generate a high point in both the quality and the quantity of morris dancing, but the concentration of collectors and researchers in this direction was balanced by a neglect of morris from elsewhere. Morris from these other areas was seen (if seen at all) as inferior and not really worth recording (time was short and was better spent in the Cotswolds). This neglect, particularly in the early years of the twentieth century when memories might still have been recoverable, has condemned Other Morris to a lowly position – lower than it deserved. It would, I think, be fair to say that interest in Other Morris did not come to life until about 1970: thus is the history of the nineteenth century affected by the interests of the twentieth.

A quick flick through the List of Morris Events, onwards from the earthquake at Grimsby in 1749, will show that although the Cotswolds lead by a big margin, there is a substantial minority of events scattered widely across the country. Most of these are too miscellaneous to merit mention in a summary such as this, but there are two groups that do hang together: the morris associated with the rush-bearing and rushcarts of Lancashire and Cheshire which, by the nature of the event, had to be processional; and the morris on London streets, which was, of course, the Cotswold dancers on tour.

So, from the time of the Verney letters and the Dixton painting, I think we can see in the Cotswold area a tradition of morris dancing that would be recognisable to us today: recognisable in kit (costume); probably with a recognisable form of the dance, and having a recognisable social interaction with the community around them. The paintings from Stowe go a long way to support this view, for they look very familiar to anyone who has watched Cotswold morris recently, and yet we know that they were painted (in 1818 and 1844) of events that were themselves a deliberate revival of the old custom of morris dancing. Thus, it seems safe to say that morris, much as we know it today, was widespread in the Cotswolds in the latter half of the eighteenth century and on into the nineteenth, although by that time it needed a bit of revival. Morris in the latter half of the sixteenth century had been attacked by Puritans: in the latter half of the nineteenth it was attacked by the temperance movement.

So much for the Cotswolds: what about elsewhere? I think we need to accept that the word 'morris' was rather more casually used in those days. I recall being told of a dance teacher from Knutsford saying of the Victorian days, "We did all sorts of dancing – yes, morris was one of them". Durgan's reference to morris in Helston, Cornwall, in 1790, could have meant almost anything. The only picture we have from a non-Cotswold region that gives us a clear view of the event is the one from Failsworth near Manchester, of circa 1820. Here we have a neat set of six dancers, looking very like Cotswold, and no sign of the large numbers of dancers reported in the written sources from Lancashire. How accurate was the artist? Had Cotswold ideas spread? Our modern ideas of what is, and what is not morris, and what is, and what is not Cotswold, are no more than that – just modern ideas. A couple of centuries ago people wouldn't have thought such thoughts, and didn't much care.

At the risk of writing a summary of a summary, it seems clear that what we would all recognise as morris dancing goes back to the early eighteenth century. Then for the three hundred years before that, we see the word morris in fairly regular use but applied to styles of performance about which we know very little. However, one thing is very clear: those emotive words 'pagan', 'ritual', 'pre-Christian' and 'fertility rite' make no appearance at all, for these are ideas of the twentieth century put forward to add colour to a revival movement and to match the romanticism that followed the First World War.

Anyone who has come forward at a morris display to address the general public will appreciate that a certain amount of fantasy goes down very well. I think it was Roy Dommett who once said, "Don't allow your story to be inhibited by the truth". What we all need to remember is that fact and fantasy are both good – we just need to remember which is which.

POSTSCRIPT

In the 2004 issue of the *Folk Music Journal* Michael Heaney reports some recent finds under the title, 'The Earliest Reference to the Morris Dance?'

From 19 May 1448, in the accounts of the Worshipful Company of Goldsmiths (London) –

Item to the Moryssh dancers   7s.

It is noteworthy that this clearly relates to an actual performance, whereas the Wetenhale Will shows morris used as a design motif.

An inventory of Caistor Castle in Norfolk, dated 31 October 1448, mentions a tapestry depicting a morysk dance. (There are similar mentions, presumably of the same tapestry, in two other inventories, one of 1462 and one undated.) It is reasonable to assume that both the purchaser and the weaver knew something about morris.

These new discoveries extend the history of morris dancing in England by ten years but, fortunately, they do not seriously undermine any of the views already expressed.